CONTINUUM READER'S GUIDES

Achebe's Things Fall Apart – Ode Ogede

William Blake's Poetry – Jonathan Roberts

Chaucer's The Canterbury Tales – Gail Ashton

Conrad's Heart of Darkness – Allan Simmons

Dickens's Great Expectations – Ian Brinton

Fitzgerald's The Great Gatsby – Nicolas Tredell

Salinger's The Catcher in the Rye – Sarah Graham

FOWLES'S
THE FRENCH LIEUTENANT'S WOMAN

WILLIAM STEPHENSON

continuum

Continuum

The Tower Building
11 York Road
London
SE1 7NX

80 Maiden Lane
Suite 704
New York
NY 10038

www.continuumbooks.com

British Library Cataloguing-in-Publication Data
A catalogue record for this book is available from the British Library.

ISBN-10: HB: 0-8264-9008-5
PB: 0-8264-9009-3
ISBN-13: HB: 978-0-8264-9008-7
PB: 978-0-8264-9009-4

Library of Congress Cataloging-in-Publication Data
Stephenson, William, 1965–
Fowles's The French Lieutenant's Woman / William Stephenson.
p. cm.
Includes bibliographical references.
ISBN-13: 978-0-8264-9008-7
ISBN-10: 0-8264-9008-5
ISBN-13: 978-0-8264-9009-4
ISBN-10: 0-8264-9009-43
1. Fowles, John, 1926–2005. French Lieutenant's Woman. 2. Fowles, John, 1926–2005—Technique. 3. Fowles, John, 1926–2005—Film and video adaptations. I. Title.

PR6056.O85F73 2007
823'.914—dc22
2007008728

Typeset by Servis Filmsetting Ltd, Manchester
Printed and bound in Great Britain by
Cromwell Press Ltd, Trowbridge, Wiltshire

CONTENTS

To Anna and Aidan

ACKNOWLEDGEMENTS

I would like to thank Sarah Fowles and the John Fowles estate for giving permission to quote from his work, and Random House for the right to use their editions. I am indebted to Continuum, particularly Anna Sandeman for commissioning this study, and making helpful suggestions as editor, and Colleen Coalter for her help with administration. Thanks also go to Marianne Colbran and Phil Barden for assisting with research on the reviews of *The French Lieutenant's Woman*. I am grateful, as ever, to my colleagues at the University of Chester for useful insights, and those students on the Postmodern and Contemporary Literature and Modernism and After modules who taught me so much about Fowles's novel.

ABBREVIATIONS OF WORKS CITED

A	John Fowles, *The Aristos* (revised edition) (1981, London: Triad Grafton)
AM	John Fowles, *A Maggot* (1996, London: Vintage)
C	John Fowles, *The Collector* (1998, London: Vintage)
Con	Dianne L. Vipond (ed.), *Conversations with John Fowles* (1999, Jackson, MS: University Press of Mississippi)
DM	John Fowles, *Daniel Martin* (1998, London: Vintage)
ET	John Fowles, *The Ebony Tower* (1997, London: Vintage)
FLW	John Fowles, *The French Lieutenant's Woman* (1996, London: Vintage)
I	John Fowles, *Islands* (1978, London: Jonathan Cape)
J I	John Fowles, *The Journals, Volume 1*, ed. Charles Drazin (2003, London: Jonathan Cape)
J II	John Fowles, *The Journals, Volume 2*, ed. Charles Drazin (2006, London: Jonathan Cape)
M	John Fowles, *The Magus: A Revised Version* (1997, London: Vintage)
S	Harold Pinter, *The French Lieutenant's Woman: A Screenplay* (1981, Boston, MA, Toronto: Little Brown)
T	John Fowles, *The Tree* (2000, London: Vintage)
G	John Fowles, 'Thank the gods for bloody mindedness', *Guardian*, 28 May 1992, 25
W	John Fowles, *Wormholes: Essays and Occasional Writings*, ed. Jan Relf (1999, London: Vintage)

CHAPTER 1

CONTEXTS

AUTHOR AND INFLUENCES

Few novelists are able to enjoy commercial success *and* critical esteem in any measure, but during his long life, John Fowles managed both. His fiction posed philosophical problems about individuality, sexuality, creativity, ecology and many other issues, but artfully concealed them beneath the suspense and eroticism of popular forms like the thriller and the romance, from which he borrowed unstintingly. His first novel, *The Collector* (1963), was a parable of the confrontation between reactionary ignorance and progressive self-awareness, symbolized by the kidnapping of a beautiful young art student by a repressed council worker, but was read by most people as a straightforward crime story. His second, *The Magus* (1965), was an existentialist tale of personal growth, framed as a series of intellectual and sexual games played on a young man by a mysterious millionaire on a Greek island, assisted by glamorous twin sisters. Both were bestsellers. After the publication of Fowles's third novel, *The French Lieutenant's Woman*, in 1969, critics called him the paradigm of a new postmodernist generation, audacious enough to acknowledge his debt to past literature by playing irreverent formal games with its most cherished conventions. Their analysis, remarkably, was applied to a novel that remained on the *New York Times* and *Time* magazine bestseller lists for more than a year. It also won the W. H. Smith & Son prize in 1970 and the Silver PEN Award in 1969, respectively reflecting mainstream approval and the admiration of fellow novelists. *The French Lieutenant's Woman* was soon recognized as Fowles's most important work.

Fowles was born on 31 March 1926, in Leigh-on-Sea, Essex. His father, Robert Fowles, was a tobacco importer, and his mother Gladys (née Richards) a housewife. Until the outbreak of the Second World War, John's childhood was ordinary and suburban. In the 1940s and 1950s, he attended Bedford School, served as a lieutenant in the Royal Marines, read Modern Languages at New College, Oxford, worked and travelled in France, Greece and elsewhere, then finally returned to England to teach and write.

Along the way, he was absorbing influences that began well before the twentieth century. As a child he had been enraptured by *Bevis* by Richard Jeffries, a Victorian account of an adventurous rural boyhood, and 'the first book that I ever loved passionately and almost totally lived [. . .] a unique master-influence' (*W*, 36). During the Blitz, at the age of 14, he was evacuated to Ipplepen, an idyllic village in Devon. There, the passionate imaginings inspired by *Bevis* became real: reading and experience fused to give Fowles a lifelong interest in nature both in the botanical sense and as a theme. Ipplepen was recreated in the opening chapter of his 1977 novel *Daniel Martin*, where the young protagonist 'comes each spring to find the first moschatel [. . .] Another mystery, his current flower and emblem' (*DM*, 16). Like Daniel, Fowles returned to Ipplepen each year during the school holidays, as his parents had moved there, to re-immerse himself in the rural landscape, a constant source of adventure and surprise, which stimulated him to write: he began his first composition, a nature journal, in December 1941 (Warburton, 2004, 31).

Fowles went on to write several non-fiction pieces about nature and ecology. In the most substantial of these, *The Tree*, he argued that the fundamental setting of all literature from the ancient epics onwards was a journey through an unknown forest, typified by the woods of the Arthurian legends: 'the metaphorical forest is constant suspense, stage awaiting actors: heroes, maidens, dragons, mysterious castles at every step' (*T*, 64). Fowles was connecting his love for nature with another strong source of imaginative energy, the medieval romances he had read while studying French at university. As he said in a note to his own translation of *Eliduc*, one of the twelfth-century *Lais* of Marie de France, although the novelist may feel condescension towards such seemingly simple medieval tales, 'I do not think any writer of fiction can do so with decency' because 'He is watching his own birth' (*ET*, 119). In Fowles's view, the *Lais* were both conservative and experimental. Marie de France leaned heavily on the *Matière de Bretagne* (the cycle of the Arthurian legends), which was traditional even at the time she wrote. However, Marie's work was characterized by 'sexual honesty and a very feminine awareness of how people really behave – and how behaviour and moral problems can be expressed through things such as dialogue and action' (*W*, 185). This led Fowles to link her to a more recent female writer, Jane Austen, whose texts were also 'formal as tapestries at one moment, as natural as life the next' (*W*, 183). Fowles's art was thus born of two parents: the formulaic, fantastical medieval romance, and the structurally more flexible, emotionally subtler tradition of nineteenth-century realism. His fiction retained the narrative vigour of the older form while infusing it with a much subtler content and making it psychologically plausible, echoing 'the transmutation that took place when Marie grafted her own knowledge of the world onto the old material' (*W*,185).

GENESIS AND COMPOSITION

The French Lieutenant's Woman enriched Fowles's characteristic mixture of romance and realism by using a historical setting seen from the perspective of a contemporary narrator. Fowles chose to set the story in 1867–9, exactly a century before the composition of the book, and therefore in Victorian England, where the social conventions governing love, sexuality, religion and class were radically different from those of his own time (even if, as we will see, many of the underlying issues were very similar). As if to emphasize the novel's distance from its Victorian setting, the modern narrator comments ironically on the action, just as Marie de France's narrator did with the traditional Arthurian material she reworked.

The French Lieutenant's Woman's basic structure is a very old one, derived from the archetypal romance plot of the meeting, separation and reunion of two lovers. Charles Smithson is a nobleman and amateur scientist who is engaged to the *nouveau riche* Ernestina Freeman, heiress to the fortune of her father, a successful retailer. Sarah Woodruff is a former governess reduced to employment as a companion (effectively a servant) to the odious Mrs Poulteney. On holiday with Ernestina in Lyme Regis, Charles sees Sarah staring out to sea on the Cobb, or harbour breakwater. She is known locally as a fallen woman because of a past affair with Varguennes, a shipwrecked sailor, which allegedly led to her losing her virginity and has thus ruined her reputation, leading the locals to nickname her 'the French lieutenant's whore'. Despite the difference in their backgrounds, and the danger of being seen, Charles and Sarah meet several times in a secluded wooded area, the Undercliff, to the west of Lyme. Charles falls in love with Sarah and offers to help her. Sarah leaves Lyme for Exeter. Charles follows her there and has sex with her in a hotel room. Even though he discovers Sarah has been lying to him about Varguennes, and was a virgin, he breaks off his engagement to Ernestina. He is disgraced after Sam, his servant, tells Ernestina's father about the affair. Charles returns to Exeter, intending to marry Sarah, only to find she has vanished. He leaves England for America, but after two years, Sarah is discovered in London, living as a model and amanuensis to Dante Gabriel Rossetti. When Charles and Sarah meet again, the novel famously divides into two endings, the closed one of chapter 60 where they form a reunited family (because in this ending their single sexual encounter has produced a daughter), and the open one of chapter 61 in which Sarah rejects Charles's offer of marriage and he returns to America alone, but with the chance of leading a free, existentially authentic life.

Such a bald summary can only suggest the barest outline of the novel's main story. There are also sub-plots; digressions by the narrator; miniature essays on sexuality, evolution and religion; descriptive passages; dialogues; footnotes; formal experiments; extended quotations, and allusions. These will be addressed in later chapters. For now, it is important to set the novel in context, by concentrating on Fowles's relationship to his work. Despite the novel's historical setting, it had its genesis not in a documented event but in a picture that came to Fowles's mind in late 1966, when he was in the middle of working on another project:

> A woman stands at the end of a deserted quay and stares out to sea. That was all. [. . .] These mythopoeic 'stills' (they seem almost always static) float into my mind very often. I ignore them, since that is the best way of finding whether they really are the door into a new world. (*W*, 14)

When Fowles first conceived her, the woman on the quay was from no particular historical period. Instead, she was 'a figure from myth' (*FLW*, 11), drawn from Fowles's knowledge of those literary heroines whose role is to pine for absent sailors, from ancient epic poetry onwards: 'The first novel in world literature is woven of islands and the sea, and of solitude and sexuality' (*I*, 51). Fowles refers to Homer's *Odyssey*, in which several women, notably Penelope and Calypso, love the missing Odysseus. Not coincidentally, the voyage was one of Fowles's favoured metaphors for literary composition. He believed that when writing, any novelist must set forth 'into the unknown of his own unconscious', and can only hope to find 'a wise Penelope waiting at the end' (*I*, 74). Given these remarks, and Fowles's comments about the origin of his art in French romances such as *Eliduc*, Sarah's staring out over the sea suggests not only the character's pining for her absent lover but also Fowles's compositional focus on the voyage into the unknown, and his intertextual gaze towards the *Matière de Bretagne*. Indeed, the ship that brought Varguennes hailed from Saint Malo, a Breton port (*FLW*, 37). *The French Lieutenant's Woman* was a love story, but also a meditation upon composition: 'a first-person novel about the creative process, disguised as a third-person Victorian romance' (Warburton, 2004, 294).

The composition of *The French Lieutenant's Woman* was long and arduous. The novel was released in Britain on 12 June 1969. Fowles had begun writing it on 25 January 1967, soon after the arrival of the mental image of the woman on the quay. Fowles was then living in Underhill Farm, an old building in the woods to the west of Lyme Regis. The narrator suggests 'perhaps I now live in one of the houses I have brought into the fiction' (*FLW*, 97): this was indeed the case for Fowles, as Underhill Farm became the Dairy, one of the last buildings on the fringes of Lyme before the wildness of the Undercliff. The Dairy is represented as 'a long thatched cottage' with 'two or three meadows round it, running down to the cliffs' (87) and it has a local reputation for its cream and butter; even the outsider Charles has heard of it (88). This suggests a personal joke by Fowles about his fame as the writer of two bestselling novels, churning out fictions just like the dairy-man, a 'vast-bearded man with a distinctly saturnine cast' who enjoys spreading malicious rumours, calls Sarah a whore, and seems to Charles 'to incarnate all the hypocritical gossip' of Lyme (88, 89). Fowles certainly did have a cottage industry going at the Farm: even while he was drafting *The French Lieutenant's Woman*, he managed, with staggering stamina, also to write an as yet unpublished thriller of 110,000 words.

Despite such distractions, he completed the second draft of *The French Lieutenant's Woman* and presented it to his wife Elizabeth on 17 June 1968. She suggested several important amendments. As one of Fowles's handwritten notes on the man-uscript stated, Elizabeth was his 'sternest editor' (Mansfield, 1981, 278 n.). Because of her interventions, Fowles removed several didactic or redundant passages. Elizabeth also disap-proved of the single, closed ending her husband had offered. Consequently, he evolved the now familiar double ending in July 1968: however, when he sent the manuscript of the third draft to Tom Maschler, his editor at Jonathan Cape, the more conven-tional, closed chapter was placed last. Maschler suggested the final order (*Con*, 127), thus leaving the novel poised between alternative conclusions, but with Charles's lonely voyage away from Sarah situated last, preventing the comfortably closed ending from assuming 'the tyranny of the last chapter, the final, the "real" version' (*FLW*, 390).

In this way, the structure of the novel echoes its existentialist ide-ology. The endings and their order imply that existential freedom is always a choice, an ever-present alternative to social convention, and the continuous possibility of this choice cannot, or should not, allow conformist, dutiful behaviour to have the final say, or conclude anyone's inner narrative. Instead, people must constantly choose between the straitjacket of society and their individual freedom, which can be terrifying and chaotic: 'life[. . .] is to be, however inadequately, emptily, hopelessly [. . .] endured' (*FLW*, 445).

Such advice was ironically appropriate. At the time of composition and submission of the manuscript, Fowles's life was in disorder. Although he was a commercially successful writer, he resented losing most of his earnings in tax, and was seriously considering financial exile abroad by early 1968, at which point nature intervened: the seaward fields beyond Underhill Farm collapsed in an overnight landslip on 24 February, forcing the Fowleses to sell the property (Warburton, 2004, 300–04). They eventually rejected the plan to live abroad, and in January 1969 moved to Belmont House, a larger and more geologically secure property above the town. Amid the chaos of emptying Underhill Farm and jettisoning most of their possessions, Fowles sent the manuscript to Tom Maschler on 5 September 1968, with the caveat 'You won't like it' (Warburton, 2004, 305). Fowles's pessimism was unjustified. Maschler called it 'magnificent' (*J II*, 47) and it secured Fowles's literary reputation (see Chapter 4).

EXISTENTIALISM AND POSTMODERNISM

The French Lieutenant's Woman, like Fowles's art as a whole, emerged from his engagement with ideas. Although any list of such ideas is bound to be reductive, it is fair to say that Fowles's work has a number of consistent concerns. Among these are: man's relationship to nature; class and social hierarchy; sex and gender roles; authorship and the creative process; the power of unexplained mystery; existentialism; and postmodernism. The later chapters will refer to all of these, but here it is necessary to focus on the last two, because if *The French Lieutenant's Woman* can be summed up in a sentence, it is a postmodernist development of the existentialist blueprint of Fowles's earlier novels. (These novels, and Fowles's early non-fiction text, *The Aristos*, are referred to in Chapter 6.) Existentialism was an individualist philosophy, based on the idea that it is every human being's personal responsibility to create their own authentic selfhood, rather than accepting a model handed down by, say, family, society or religion. Fowles defined existentialism as 'the revolt of the individual against all those systems of thought, theories of psychology, and social and political pressures that attempt to rob him of his individuality' (*A*, 115). Fowles's interest in it emerged from his early encounters with the French existentialists Jean-Paul Sartre and Albert Camus, whose work he had read extensively as a young man (*Con*, 88). Fowles articulated *The French Lieutenant's Woman*'s relationship to existentialism in his notes written during the novel's composition, which were published as 'Notes on an Unfinished Novel' (1969):

> My two previous novels were both based on more or less disguised existentialist premises. I want this one to be no exception; and so I am trying to show an existentialist awareness before it was chronologically possible. Kierkegaard was, of course, totally unknown to the British and American Victorians; but it has always seemed to me that the Victorian age, especially from 1850 on, was highly existentialist in many of its personal dilemmas. (*W*, 18)

Fowles used the novel's 1860s setting to comment on 1960s issues, such as the problem of whether the individual can, or ought to, break free of social convention in order to form their own identity (see 'The Social Context' below). Thus his novel queried the complacent stereotype that the twentieth century was more sophisticated or thoughtful than its predecessor. Indeed, he even reversed the relationship, suggesting that the existentialist writers who influenced him were in effect aiming to impart a 'Victorian seriousness of purpose and moral sensitivity' (*W*, 19). This attitude remained consistent throughout his working life. In a 1995 interview, when asked about his preference for novelistic content over form, he replied that he hankered after the 'Victorian attitude' of preferring serious content to perfect form (*W*, 443).

In keeping with its focus on the basic existentialist dilemma of whether to live within or outside social norms, *The French*

Lieutenant's Woman has an ambiguous relationship to the cultural conventions that inform it, chief among which is postmodernism, arguably the dominant cultural movement of the late twentieth century. Postmodernism is more difficult to define than existentialism (and in fact, *resists* definition as imposing an outdated form of conceptual closure): it has been defined in almost as many ways as there are writers upon it. It is supposed to suggest incredulity towards the grand narratives of history, philosophy and religion upon which Western culture is based, and which claim to offer some final truth or revealed knowledge (Lyotard, 1984); it may refer to a culture in which the image or simulacrum has become so dominant and all-pervading that no original reality can be said to exist any more (Baudrillard, 1994); or it may be a mere expression of the current economic base, the cultural logic of late capitalism (Jameson, 1991). *The French Lieutenant's Woman* is in many ways not a postmodernist novel at all. Seemingly postmodernist tricks, such as the flagrant manipulation of the story by the narrator, are found in the Victorian fiction that the novel imitates; also, the novel's ambiguously framed but consistent focus on the quest of the male protagonist for personal freedom suggests a modernist *Bildungsroman* akin to those of D. H. Lawrence or James Joyce (see Chapter 2). Fowles himself was allied to a psychological model of creativity that ignored postmodernist scepticism and placed great faith in the grand narratives of Freudian and Jungian psychoanalysis. He saw literary composition as 'an interior voyage of epic proportions' in which 'the psychic sailor, implicitly male, encounters a series of female archetypes' (Stephenson, 2003, 44).

Despite this, critics have read *The French Lieutenant's Woman* as a postmodernist text since the 1980s (see Chapter 4). It conforms to the stereotype of postmodernist writing in that it blurs the boundary between literature and popular fiction: it uses an extensive vocabulary, engages with philosophy and literary theory, and yet relies on popular conventions, such as dealing with separate plots in alternating chapters to increase suspense, and the gradual heightening of erotic tension until the obligatory sex scene. Moreover, like a typical postmodernist novel, it does not pretend to have made a radical break with the past (as modernist literature tried to do): postmodernist critics have focused particularly on *The French Lieutenant's Woman*'s playful acknowledgement of its literary and historical sources, achieved without simple mockery or the complacent assumption of originality. In *A Poetics of Postmodernism*, Linda Hutcheon coined the term 'historiographic metafiction' to encompass novels like *The French Lieutenant's Woman*. Her account of the novel made it an exemplar of postmodernism:

> In most of the critical work on postmodernism, it is narrative – be it in literature, history, or theory – that has usually been the major focus of attention. Historiographic metafiction incorporates all three of these domains: that is, its theoretical self-awareness of history and fiction as human constructs (historio*graphic meta*fiction) is made the grounds for its rethinking and reworking of the forms and contents of the past. (Hutcheon, 1988, 5; emphasis in original)

The French Lieutenant's Woman is a historiographic metafiction insofar as it openly imitates the styles, forms and other devices of Victorian novels, in a way that acknowledges how derivative it actually is. Through such devices as the dual ending and the conspicuous interventions of the narrator, it exposes itself as fiction rather than a historical document, and exposes the basis of history in narrative; and yet it situates itself as a document of its own time, the 1960s, when it makes reference to some of the controversial ideas about literature and society that were emerging when it was published.

THE SOCIAL CONTEXT

The 1960s were a time of international upheaval. The Berlin Wall had been built; Soviet cosmonauts had become the first human beings to venture into space; nuclear war had been narrowly averted after the Cuban missile crisis; John F. Kennedy and Martin Luther King had been assassinated; the Civil Rights Act had been passed in the USA, making racial discrimination illegal; and the Vietnam War had escalated into a vast conflict that polarized the American nation and ignited global controversy. In Britain, the ruling establishment found itself besieged by a loose alliance between consumerism, increasing disrespect for the prevailing class hierarchy, the women's movement, the dawning sexual revolution and the gradual emergence of a post-colonial multicultural society. The evidence of change was clear. During the 1960s, D. H. Lawrence's sexually explicit novel *Lady Chatterley's Lover* had been prosecuted for obscenity but cleared by the jury; National Service (armed forces conscription for young men) had been abolished; the Commonwealth Immigration Act had placed restrictions upon entry into the UK for British subjects from former colonies such as Nigeria, Kenya, Tanzania and the Gambia (all of which had become independent during the decade); the contraceptive pill had become available on the National Health Service; the death penalty had been abolished by Parliament; the psychedelic drug LSD became widely used and was then made illegal; abortion and homosexuality were both effectively legalized; Britain appointed its first female judge; and the critic Kenneth Tynan became the first person to say 'fuck' on British television.

In Fowles's obituary in the *Guardian*, John Ezard set *The French Lieutenant's Woman* in the context of the 1960s, by pointing out how the popularity of a text with such experimental features arose from the sense of social change prevailing at the time: 'Its year of publication, like the period in which it was set, was a time in which people felt they sensed the tectonic plates of change shifting under their feet' (Ezard, 2005). By 1969, Fowles, who was then in his early forties, had a clear sense of the generation gap, and knew which side of it he was on:

> the younger generation today [. . .] have rejected culture, book culture especially, and they embrace direct experience, doing your thing, finding your own scene and all the rest of the cant phrases. (*J II*, 65)

Fowles reflected that he was not entirely against such spontaneity, but feared that younger people would lose touch with traditional culture and be unable to regain it when older. Given Fowles's sensitivity to social division, it is not surprising that *The French Lieutenant's Woman* addressed tensions felt in both nineteenth- *and* twentieth-century England: the conflict between women and patriarchy; changing sexual morality; the struggle between vested interests and the ambitious working class; the challenges to the prevailing, often unspoken consensus of what constituted Englishness. The novel also struck a chord with its American audience, because 'its Undercliff setting echoed the longings of the 1960s youth counterculture' for a rural recreation of Eden, and 'it dramatized youthful outsiders challenging a society's staid conventions'. Moreover, Sarah's proto-feminist struggle for independence 'was hotly affirmed in the imaginations of thousands of women' (Warburton, 2004, 317).

Like the society that spawned it, *The French Lieutenant's Woman* asserted its progress beyond the past, and yet looked back to it continually. The structure of the novel, which dissects the anatomy of realist illusion through the various intrusions by the narrator, especially where he decides the order of the endings by tossing a coin (see Chapter 2), represents more than just a challenge to literary convention. The grand narrative of imperial history had fallen apart: nineteenth-century Britain's sense of steady progress towards global domination had been devastated by two world wars, and the aftershocks were being felt at just the time Fowles wrote. Nevertheless, Britain's concept of itself was still intimately related, however misguidedly, to a past imperial and therefore Victorian model. *The French Lieutenant's Woman* cleverly addressed this national self-concept by acknowledging the continuing dependency of its own time upon Victorian tradition, and yet exposing that relationship to irony without complacently assuming the superiority of the present. On his birthday, 31 March 1969, three months before the novel was published, Fowles wrote in his journal:

I really do see them all [anniversaries] as tribal, neolithic, runestone rubbish. I watched Eisenhower's funeral for a time this evening; that too is neolithic – much nearer painting oneself with red ochre than to the age of Apollo Nine. (*J II*, 58)

Fowles astutely acknowledged the awkward balance in 1960s culture between a sense of progress through scientific exploration (the climax of the space race: astronauts were to land on the moon within four months) and the need to cling to atavistic ritual (the stage-managed funeral of the warrior chieftain: Eisenhower was a general of the Second World War who became President of the USA). Not coincidentally, it was contemporary information technology, the television, which allowed Fowles to make the connection in the first place.

The French Lieutenant's Woman also fitted the mood of the times when it combined the popular and experimental. Through refusing to maintain a veneer of realist illusion or to end in a decorous Victorian manner, it challenged the narratives handed down to it that explained how things ought to be (and how stories ought to end). At the same time, though, it retained many of the characteristic features of great nineteenth-century novels. These included a dominant narrative voice, a story of love hindered by the class system, and an account of an independent woman's effort to overcome the trials forced on her by gender (all of which apply as much to canonical fictions like Charlotte Brontë's *Jane Eyre* or Jane Austen's *Pride and Prejudice*, as to Fowles's text).

The French Lieutenant's Woman engaged with the challenges faced by the 1960s by suggesting how similar they were to Victorian problems, even in incidental references to the urban environment: 'Mid-Victorian traffic-jams were quite as bad as modern ones' (280). As Charles progresses through a busy London street, 'an image-boy' runs up to him, hawking a sheet of coloured prints (281). Like the postmodern society heralded by Baudrillard, then, Victorian capitalism was sustained by the commodification of the image. As well as anxieties about technology, the novel addressed deeper underlying problems, such as threats to the prevailing social order. Charles feels redundant as a gentleman, part of a doomed class, when he unhappily notes the vitality of the working class people around him in London. Typically, he sees his own redundancy in Darwinian terms: 'the brisker and fitter forms of life jostled busily before him, like pond amoeba under a microscope' (281). Charles's anxiety reflects the reactionary fear of modernity felt by the 1960s

British establishment. For example, Alan Sinfield argues that Desmond Morris's sociological text *The Naked Ape* (first published 1967) was an instance of the establishment thinking of constructed human nature as essentially bestial, and social organization as fundamentally primitive: society is 'in reality [. . .] an incredibly complicated series of interlocking and overlapping tribal groups' (Morris, cited in Sinfield, 2004, 168). According to Sinfield, one effect of this theory of a savage human nature was that socially inferior tribes needed to be policed: 'all kinds of restrictions and controls are necessary: it helps to legitimate authoritarian attitudes' (169).

The French Lieutenant's Woman exposed establishment authoritarianism at work a century earlier, arising from a similar fear of the primitive origins of man, and his alleged innate aggression. The Victorian opponents of Darwin believed that if his theory of the survival of the fittest were applied to society, morality would become 'hypocrisy' and duty 'a straw hut in a hurricane' (*FLW*, 119). The establishment used Christianity as a means of countering this threat: the arch-capitalist Mr Freeman contributes 'handsomely' to the Society for the Propagation of Christian Knowledge and similar organizations. His workers 'were atrociously lodged and exploited by our standards' but by those of 1867 his firm is a model of philanthropic excellence, and he knows his heirs will profit from a happy labour force (272). His philanthropy is essentially a reactive attempt to control the subversive potential of the proletariat – a defence against the nightmare of social Darwinism. As he tells Charles, 'This is a great age of progress. And progress is like a lively horse. Either one rides it, or it rides one' (278). Malcolm Bradbury pinpointed this sense of the challenge of progress felt in the mid–late nineteenth century:

> The time seemed one of those phases in history when the past no longer might hand on its vision to the present; where the new generation were initiated into mysteries and experiences that their predecessors could not understand. The sense of historical 'jump' produced a reaching of the imagination out beyond the existing frames of thought and the existing forms of society. The mental set of the past was no longer acceptable;

but what, in a secular and increasingly rational universe, were the new myths, the new meanings? (Bradbury, 1971, 60–1)

Bradbury's account could equally apply to the 1960s: *The French Lieutenant's Woman* arose as a response to the challenge of historical disjunction felt in both the Victorian and modern periods. Unlike most novels, then, it had *two* social contexts, in both of which individuals faced 'highly existentialist' personal dilemmas and in which society faced an urgent need to find 'new myths' to replace the inadequate ones it had inherited. *The French Lieutenant's Woman* was an attempt to answer the questions posed by two superficially different but fundamentally similar centuries.

CHAPTER 2

LANGUAGE, STYLE AND FORM

The French Lieutenant's Woman is a mixture of contradictions. It reads like a Victorian novel yet at other times like a postmodernist one, often in the same paragraph; it shows affectionate irony towards its sources but occasionally mocks them; it flaunts its literariness and yet devotes whole chapters to historical or psychological essays; it exploits the love-triangle convention of popular fiction, and yet refuses to resolve Charles and Sarah's romance, because of its two endings (let alone the false ending in Chapter 44, in which Charles marries Ernestina). This chapter will consider three significant elements of the novel that give it its distinctive balance between contemporary experimentation and imitation of the nineteenth-century canon. These are the narrative voice, the dual ending, and the text's mixture of modern and Victorian styles and ideas. These elements are connected: it is the narrator who initiates the dual ending by turning back his watch 15 minutes in the final chapter; he generally adopts the idiom of a Victorian omniscient storyteller, but at other times takes on the style of a hundred years later, especially when he refers to the existential freedom of the protagonists and his consequent lack of control over them. It is very important that *The French Lieutenant's Woman* refuses to resolve most of these contradictions: the reader is given the freedom to decide which is the most significant ending (if either), whether and where to believe the narrator, and so on. Likewise, the text's juxtapositions of contemporary and nineteenth-century ways of writing and thinking usually remain unresolved, and instead they are left in creative tension: this chapter explores this productive balance, using a model taken from the Russian formalist critic Mikhail Bakhtin. The chapter concludes with a look at two further passages in order to explore how they might be read with special attention to language and structure.

THE NARRATIVE VOICE

The narrator personifies many of the novel's contradictions. He usually comments on the action from outside, but twice enters the story: first, when he shares a train compartment with Charles; and second, when he drives up to Sarah's house in his coach. He imitates the omniscience of Victorian narrators when he adopts an all-knowing and all-seeing vantage point (as used by, say, George Eliot and Thomas Hardy). At other times, though, he refuses to enter the consciousness of the main characters on the grounds that they have, and deserve, existential freedom. Like Sarah Woodruff, he can be 'described only by oxymoron; luring-receding, subtle-simple, proud-begging, defending-accusing' (*FLW*, 328). Chapter 13 is his biggest scene, where he intrudes to address the reader directly, breaking the flow of the plot and thus vividly demonstrating his authority over the text, only to tell us that he cannot control his characters. He claims that he does not know why Sarah, Charles and the others act or what they will do, because he has broken the Victorian convention that the novelist stands next to God – or rather, he represents a new kind of God, whose work is based on freedom: 'There is only one good definition of God: the freedom that allows other freedoms to exist' (99). The narrator protests against the idea that literary characters should be obedient self-analysts, each ready with 'a thorough analysis of their motives and intentions' (97). Neither the characters nor the narrator will conform to such an image. Instead, Chapter 13 offers a parody by the narrator of such self-analysis, an examination of the creative process that offers important insights and yet subverts itself when the narrator claims that 'Fiction is woven into all' (99), including our daily thoughts and memories, and therefore the boundary between the real and the imaginary (or between author and novel, or narrator and story) cannot be drawn accurately.

The narrator claims that 'We are all in flight from the real reality. That is a basic definition of *Homo sapiens*' (99). This is close to the postmodernist argument, championed by Jean Baudrillard, that in the contemporary period, the idea of a 'real reality' can be treated only with ironic distance. In the postmodern era, the image 'has no relation to any reality whatsoever: it is its own pure simulacrum' (Baudrillard, 1994, 6) and it is therefore no longer possible to separate the original from the copy, or the object from the image, as the distinction has become irrelevant, and we live in age of hyper-reality, or the dominance of simulation over the supposedly 'real'. The narrator raises this issue with the reader, when he dismisses claims that Chapter 13 is absurd because the narrator cannot possibly give freedom to his characters, who, after all, are merely fictional. Instead, he argues, we all gild and censor our memorized past, to create our own 'romanced autobiography' (99): in other words, *all* human identity, not just that of literary characters, is based on fiction.

The narrator begins knowingly to expose how he creates his own identity in just such a way, by presenting a distorted and sometimes plainly false picture of his own capabilities. Chapter 13, his metafictional detour about novel-writing, ends when he returns to the position of observer by declaring that 'I report, then, only the outward facts' (99). The narrator's relegation of himself to the level of reporter is disingenuous. Although he claims that he cannot enter Sarah's consciousness or examine her motivations, he tells the reader that she 'was living in a kind of long fall' (99) and concludes the chapter by extending his metaphor:

> Charles's down-staring face had shocked her; she felt the speed of her fall accelerate; when the cruel ground rushes up, when the fall is from such a height, what use are precautions? (100)

So almost immediately after claiming that he will merely cite 'facts', the narrator fashions a biblically-based conceit, in which Sarah's metaphorical fall is not only the sexual error of a

Victorian fallen woman but also Eve's original sin. The effect is ironic: the narrator refuses the persona of an omniscient Victorian storyteller, but shows that his own existentialist, freedom-giving substitute for this persona should not be taken at face value, as he is just as happy to impose ideas on his characters as to let them form their own. As Fowles states in his notes on the novel, '*You* [the narrator] *are not the "I" who breaks into the illusion, but the "I" who is a part of it*' (*W*, 20: emphasis in original).

To interpret the narrator as simply a mouthpiece for Fowles, then, is to misunderstand the text. The narrator mockingly offers a series of possible explanations for the creative process, none of which can adequately account for the novel:

> perhaps I am writing a transposed autobiography; [. . .] perhaps Charles is myself disguised. Perhaps it is only a game. [. . .] Or perhaps I am trying to pass off a concealed book of essays on you. (97)

This is not the opinion of the real Fowles: instead of one seriously stated view of creativity, the narrator offers several comically inadequate and mutually contradictory possibilities, and whether Fowles actually believed in any of them is almost beside the point. Instead, it is the reader, rather than the characters, who is given freedom to act as he or she wants by accepting or dismissing the narrator's games.

Such games are not as original as they appear. Victorian narrators, in fact, played the same tricks. After several pages of description of a rural scene, one such narrator tells us:

> Ah, my arms are really benumbed. I have been pressing my elbows on the arms of my chair and dreaming that I was standing on the bridge in front of Dorlcote Mill as it looked one February afternoon many years ago. Before I dozed off, I was going to tell you what Mr. and Mrs. Tulliver were talking about as they sat by the bright fire in the left-hand parlour on that very afternoon I have been dreaming of. (Eliot, 1985, 55)

This is the ending to the first chapter of George Eliot's *The Mill on the Floss* (first published 1860). The narrator has already entered the consciousness of the waggoner who is 'thinking of his dinner' (54) as his horses strain up the slope towards the bridge. And yet, the little river 'seems to me like a living companion while I wander along the bank' (53): just like Fowles's narrator, who enters a railway carriage with Charles, Eliot's narrator is actually part of the scene, even though she can simultaneously tell us what characters are thinking. Even more curiously, she tells us that she has in fact been dreaming it all, showing the same daring as Fowles's narrator in the 'thoroughly traditional' but false ending of Chapter 44, where he reveals that Charles's marriage to Ernestina and Mrs. Poulteney's descent into hell were all in Charles's imagination (*FLW*, 327). In George Eliot's chapter, a little girl – later discovered to be Maggie Tulliver, the heroine – is watching the water wheel, but the narrator decides 'It is time [Maggie] went in, I think; and there is a very bright fire to tempt her' (Eliot, 1985, 55). Eliot's narrator is openly manipulating her characters, even within her supposed dream. Flagrant narratorial intrusions, then, were hardly new in the 1960s. Eliot's dream opening playfully suggests that the rest of the novel, from Mr and Mrs Tulliver's conversation onwards, might be read not as realism but as a form of oneiric vision. Eliot not only nods towards the long tradition of dream narratives in English literature (including Langland's *The Vision of Piers Plowman* and Keats's *The Fall of Hyperion: A Dream*), but also destabilizes the events of her text by exposing them as mere fiction.

This knowing, reflexive exposure of the text's intertextual links to earlier writing might be described as exemplary postmodernist technique, but for the inconvenient fact that Eliot died in 1880. In fact, this is far from the only example of a Victorian narrator intruding on the story: Robert Huffaker has pointed out that Fowles's Chapter 13 is anticipated in Chapter 15 of Anthony Trollope's *Barchester Towers* (first published 1857), where 'the novelist' breaks into the action in the first person 'to explain his views on a very important point in the art of telling tales', and in Chapter 17 of Eliot's *Adam Bede* (first published 1858), where 'the novelist' argues that life and characters should be fashioned in fiction as they are in real life (cited in Huffaker, 1980, 102). It is precisely this Victorian technique of intervention by a first-person novelist figure that Fowles is imitating in *The French Lieutenant's Woman*, even as this figure claims 'I live in the age of Alain Robbe-Grillet and Roland Barthes' (97).

THE DUAL ENDING

In the closed ending of Chapter 60, in which Charles and Sarah are reunited, *The French Lieutenant's Woman* mimics the stereotypical conclusion of a Victorian novel. After an anguished conversation, Sarah reveals to him their daughter, Lalage, and explains that everything that had happened was necessary: 'It had to be so'; Charles realizes 'it had been in God's hands, in His forgiveness of their sins' (438). They embrace and Charles asks, 'Shall I ever understand your parables?' (439). Sarah replies with a mute shake of her head. Finally, the child intervenes by banging her rag doll against Charles's cheek, to remind him 'that a thousand violins cloy very rapidly without percussion' (439). This suggests a degree of irony; however, the ending is shot through with seemingly unironic allusions to Christianity, not only in the direct mention of God, and Charles's question to Sarah about parables, but also in his realization, upon seeing her tearful, emotionally naked look at him, that 'the rock of ages can never be anything else but love' (439).

The second, open ending of Chapter 61, by contrast, gives the protagonists existential freedom, but keeps them apart. The chapter begins with a direct entry into the action by the narrator, in the guise of an overdressed impresario who turns his watch back 15 minutes, as if to permit the following scene to happen, then calls for his coach (441). Then the protagonists confront one another and do not like what they see. They stand metaphorically unclothed, in 'far less a sexual nakedness than a clinical one, one in which the hidden cancer stood revealed in all its loathsome reality' (443).

Charles realizes that Sarah is prepared to sacrifice everything but herself (443). The personal struggle of the protagonists has evolved them into existentialists, but in Sarah's case this means valuing the self not only above the laws of society, but also over the emotional claims of all others. Charles leaves angrily and takes a long, lonely walk away from Sarah, having 'at last found an atom of faith in himself, a true uniqueness, on which to build' (445). Chapter 61 is twentieth-century in form as well as content. It imitates the open, existentially free endings of canonical modernist novels. For example, D. H. Lawrence's *Sons and Lovers* (first published 1913) finishes when the protagonist Paul Morel leaves his family and lovers behind and sets off on an independent career as a painter, eager to embrace modernity: 'He walked towards the faintly humming, glowing town, quickly' (Lawrence, 1993, 446). James Joyce's *A Portrait of the Artist as a Young Man* (first published 1916) concludes similarly when the hero Stephen Dedalus abandons the repressive Catholic morality of Ireland to start a new life abroad: 'to forge in the smithy of my soul the uncreated conscience of my race' (Joyce, 2000, 213). In neither case does the reader know what new trials face the protagonist, or whether he will succeed. Charles Smithson, leaving Sarah for an uncertain future in America, has a streak of Paul and Stephen in him.

Readers' opinions of the endings vary. Some declare the second, existentialist ending the more important. Elizabeth D. Rankin argues that it plays a crucial role in exemplifying the novel's philosophy:

> without this ending – or with this ending undercut or made anti-climactic by a subsequent ending – there would be no perfect exemplar of existential freedom in the novel and hence that concept would remain hazy throughout. (Rankin, 1973, 205)

Rankin reads Chapter 61 as a practical demonstration of what, up until then, has been merely a theory: the protagonists' separation is the painful but vitally necessary realization of their aspirations to existential independence. Mahmoud Salami, by contrast, believes that the dual ending, in which neither chapter dominates, is vital to the novel's existentialist and postmodernist projects:

The novel's open-endedness is a form of freedom to Charles as well as to the reader, a factor that undermines authority in the narrative. This still life at the end of the novel reflects the free ending, the incompleteness of texts, and the deferment of their meanings. (Salami, 1992, 134)

As Salami argues, the dual ending gives the reader freedom to connect the last two chapters and make sense of the contradictions between them. Furthermore, it permits the text to display its postmodernist rejection of Victorian closure. It also has a historical function: the juxtaposition of the Victorian family of Chapter 60 with the lone hero of Chapter 61 gives the reader the opportunity to compare the modern and Victorian eras without being given clear guidance by the narrator (Salami, 1992, 133–4). Another critic has argued that the duality of the ending suggests the chance element in the evolution of the modern period out of the Victorian. Tony E. Jackson, while himself preferring the second ending, underlines the importance that the two have together. He refers to the evolutionary theorist Stephen Jay Gould's concept of contingency, which 'preserves both randomness and determinism in an unresolvable tension with each other' (Jackson, 1997, 237):

Gould cannot reverse time's arrow and show us how the same beginning can generate a different ending. Fowles, however, does just this. We have one originating reality leading by chance to two different outcomes. Each outcome retrospectively determines what the nature of Sarah had actually been. (238)

Jackson's account of the novel incorporates elements of postmodernist science, whose theories are driven by indeterminacy rather than teleology, and which explains the universe as a complex system of unresolved tensions rather than as the expression of an unvarying system of laws. Thus Sarah and Charles *may* evolve into existentialists or may not. Likewise, on a grander scale, the modern era is only one possible outcome of the Victorian, even though, from the flawed perspective of hindsight, the twentieth century may seem to be an inevitable consequence of the nineteenth.

It would be reductive to express a simple preference for one ending over the other. As has already been suggested (see Chapter 1), placing the open chapter last allows the novel to imply that for the reader, as well as the characters, existential freedom should remain a continuous possibility, an ever-present alternative to conformity. However, despite its strengths, the second ending would have been weakened if allowed to stand on its own. By showing how neither conclusion is inevitable, the dual ending allows postmodernist indeterminacy, existentialist choice and evolutionary contingency to become issues for the reader. The narrator plainly states that the duality of the endings matters more than their order, when he makes the outrageous claim to have determined the sequence of the last two chapters by tossing a coin, while sharing a train compartment with the sleeping Charles (390). The narrator's performance is a blatant display of postmodernist self-reflexivity. The first epigraph to Chapter 61 is taken from the evolutionary theorist Martin Gardner, who argues that evolution is the process by which chance and nature combine 'to create living forms better and better adapted to survive' (440). As Rankin has argued, the novel is not only referring to its protagonists' evolution, but also to itself (see Chapter 4). *The French Lieutenant's Woman* ends twice, and thereby refuses to end at all, thus announcing its evolution beyond the closed conclusions of Victorian fiction and the open endings of modernist novels.

STYLES

Fowles's dual ending also shows how the novel has evolved beyond its predecessors on the level of style, as it offers a complex collage of modern and Victorian idioms, a 'tissue of quotations' that 'blend and clash' (Barthes, 1977, 146). In *The Aristos*, Fowles argued that a distinctive personal style should *not* be seen as the mark of an artist: instead, artists should be able to deploy styles as required. Fowles went so far as to call one chapter of *The Aristos* 'The Style is Not the Man' (*A*, 191–2). The multiple styles of *The French Lieutenant's Woman* include fake Victorian idioms. While composing the novel, Fowles reflected that the real Victorian dialogue he read in his sources was 'far too close to our own [modern speech] to sound convincingly old' and that therefore he had to 'start cheating and pick out the more formal and archaic (even for 1867)' parts of real Victorian dialogue for use in his novel (*W*, 17). *The French Lieutenant's Woman* does not simply *use* modern and Victorian styles: instead, it creates imitations of these styles, which to the reader will probably *appear* convincingly Victorian or twentieth-century. The first, closed ending, for instance, creates a collage of seemingly Victorian and modern elements:

> But against his shock – what was she now, what had she become! – there rushed a surge of relief. Those eyes, that mouth, that always implicit air of defiance . . . it was all still there. She *was* the remarkable creature of his happier memories – but blossomed, realized, winged from the black pupa.
>
> For ten long moments nothing was spoken. Then she clutched her hands nervously in front of the gilt clasp and looked down.
>
> 'How came you here, Mr. Smithson?' [. . .]
>
> 'My solicitor was told you live here. I do not know by whom.' (424: emphasis in original)

The novel fakes Victorian discourse in a way that allows a convincingly nineteenth-century surface to be troubled by modern depths. In the first paragraph, the broken syntax that tracks Charles's thoughts makes the style lean towards modernist stream of consciousness (in the manner of Virginia Woolf, say): Fowles creates a form of syntactical Morse code, in which the gaps, jumps and elisions of thought are captured on the page by dots and dashes. By contrast, Sarah and Charles's conversation, with its syntactical inversions ('How came you here'), rigidly precise grammar ('I do not know by whom') and studied formality of address ('Mr Smithson') smacks of the fake Victorian dialogue referred to by Fowles in his note. Soon afterwards, this changes, when Charles fails to end four sentences in succession: 'Every month I have advertised in the hope of . . .'; 'I see you are . . .' (424). At this point, the diction remains formal, and therefore stereotypically Victorian, but the syntax edges closer to the messiness of actual speech, and therefore to a twentieth-century form of realism.

A model for the complex clash of ideas, styles and forms in *The French Lieutenant's Woman* can be found in the work of the Russian formalist critic Mikhail Bakhtin, who argues that what he calls dialogue (meaning interaction between different discourses, or ways of writing and speaking, usually associated with different social classes or ideologies) is the basis of the novel form and is what makes it distinct from drama, poetry or non-fiction: 'the style of a novel is to be found in the combination of its styles; the language of a novel is the system of its "languages" ' (Bakhtin, 1981, 262).

The French Lieutenant's Woman offers a number of such dialogues, such as: that which takes place *within* the narrator's voice between a Victorian discourse of narration through metaphor, euphemism and omniscient insight, and a twentieth-century idiom that tends to write more literally, reveals sexual content, looks back on the Victorian era with sometimes patronizing hindsight, sometimes moves into a mode close to stream of consciousness, and refers to post-Victorian figures, concepts and technologies such as Freud, repression and the cinema.

Fowles's novel offers dialogues not only between discourses, but also between historical periods and genres. The novel's dual ending, for instance, juxtaposes Victorian closure with modernist openness, and Victorian romance with existentialist *Bildungsroman*. Catherine Belsey argues that classic realist texts are characterized by '*illusionism*, narrative which leads to *closure*, and a *hierarchy of discourses* which establishes the "truth" of the story' (Belsey, 1980, 70: emphasis in original). This means that the typical Victorian novel gives the illusion of a complete, plausible world; narrative loose ends are organized and tidied away by the end; and an organizing voice (usually that of the narrator) has a privileged status relative to the voices of the characters, and ensures that the reader knows what is actually happening and what is imaginary. One of Belsey's examples

27

of classic realism is *The Mill on the Floss*. As we have already seen, George Eliot's novel is more reflexive and self-ironic than Belsey's brief typology would make it appear. As the opening to Eliot's novel suggests, Victorian realism was a convention that sometimes questioned itself by exposing the fictional basis of the world so plausibly fabricated elsewhere in the narrative. *The French Lieutenant's Woman* goes a step further, questioning not only its own organizing conventions but also the distinction between the opposing sides of the dialogues of styles, idioms and periods within it, thus undermining its own separation from its intertextual sources. In other words, because it is not easy to determine which elements of the plot, dialogue, style, and so on, are *wholly* modern or Victorian, it is difficult to declare that *The French Lieutenant's Woman* is simply twentieth-century. It *is* partly Victorian. When the narrator says 'if this is a novel, it cannot be a novel in the modern sense of the word' (97), he means not only that he is being self-consciously avant-garde by breaking some of the twentieth-century conventions of the novel (for instance, by imitating Victorian idioms and inserting self-reflexive passages) but also that his text is too close to its nineteenth-century ancestors to be neatly separated from them.

In summary, *The French Lieutenant's Woman* offers a complex mixture of modern and Victorian structures. The formal experiments of the novel, such as Chapter 13 and the dual ending, allow nineteenth and twentieth-century literary conventions to comment on one another in a productive tension. The novel also mixes contemporary and Victorian styles, again creating a dialogue between present and past, and leaving the reader plenty of room for interpretation. The next section will consider how several key passages from *The French Lieutenant's Woman* might be read, and suggest how the views of various critics can be taken into account when doing so.

PASSAGES FOR FURTHER STUDY

The opening

The start of the novel is clearly important when discussing form, style and the role of the narrator. Fowles begins the story in a leisurely, almost circumlocutory Victorian idiom, describing the weather and scenery, and piquing the reader's interest in the two walkers on the Cobb (who turn out to be Charles and Ernestina): 'a person of curiosity could at once have deduced several strong probabilities about the pair' (9). Despite his able imitation of a Victorian storyteller, he goes on to make his twentieth-century allegiance clear by judging the past according to the limitations imposed on it by history. Ernestina's brightly coloured clothes were then the height of fashion, but they

> would strike us today as distinctly strident; but the world was then in the first fine throes of the discovery of aniline dyes. And what the feminine, by way of compensation for so much else in her expected behaviour, demanded of a colour was brilliance, not discretion. (11)

Thus the narrator paradoxically distances himself from the past at the same time as imitating its writing. He goes on to pose a further problem for the reader, as the other figure on the quay (Sarah), stands staring out to sea, more like 'a living memorial to the drowned, a figure from myth, than any proper fragment of the petty provincial day' (11). She is seemingly archetypal, existing outside the opposition of Victorian past and modern present that has so far been established. Throughout the chapter, the narrator subtly suggests the basic conceptual oppositions that will drive the novel: between the nineteenth and twentieth centuries; between the power of historical circumstance and the individual's struggle to overcome it; between conventional femininity and Sarah's mysterious presence; between social expectations and sexual and psychological drives.

The chapter can be read in terms of the dialogues it sets up between Victorian and twentieth-century viewpoints and ideas. To what extent are they wholly distinct, or are they dependent on one another, or even similar? For instance, the use of fashion as an acceptable form of female expression in a patriarchal society is arguably a characteristic of the twentieth-century as well as the Victorian era. Voyeurism, or spying, is a twentieth-century theme, too, as we know from Fowles's first two novels (see Chapter 6): the references to Grogan as 'the telescopist' (10) invite comparisons with the camera eye, and thus the cinema. The reader can analyse the way in which the narrator mixes modern and Victorian styles, and begin to think about *why* he does so. By writing of the Cobb as 'pure, clean, salt, a paragon of mass' and then adding 'I exaggerate? Perhaps' (10), the narrator encourages the reader to treat his leisurely descriptive idiom with a degree of scepticism. The novel offers a facsimile of the nineteenth century, but only a conspicuously faked, disproportioned version, designed to heighten contrasts between then and today. The reader is encouraged directly to 'put [the narrator] to the test' (10). Even this early in the book, Bakhtinian dialogues are opening up between modern and Victorian ideas and ways of expression. The passage can also be read in terms of structure. If the opening chapter begins in Victorian mode, then encourages the reader to question this, what does this suggest about the plot of the novel as a whole? To what extent will the story remain Victorian, or become contemporary?

The false ending

In Chapter 44, Charles does not go to Exeter to see Sarah in the hotel, but returns instead to Lyme. The narrator decides to finish the novel here, so he tells us that Charles, after a 'night of rebellion' at Ma Terpsichore's brothel and the prostitute's room, will 'go through with his marriage to Ernestina' (319). The lives of the characters are rounded off with absurd brevity, though space is reserved for Mrs Poulteney's shock at her descent to hell, at which she can only fume: 'Lady Cotton is behind this' (326). This false ending is followed by Chapter 45, which forms a less celebrated, but equally interesting, version of Chapter 13: this time the narrator intervenes to tell us that he has been lying, because Chapter 44 was merely Charles's daydream. To justify this, the narrator even refers to his comments made in Chapter 13 about the human tendency to live inside a fictionalized mental autobiography (327).

One possible approach to take to the false ending is a comparative one. It would need to be held up against Chapters 13, 60 and 61 in order to judge it against the earlier intervention by the narrator, and the closed and open alternative endings of the last two chapters. Thus the false ending can form an important part of a formalist reading of the novel: how does it contribute to the structure? By rendering *all* closure absurd, does Chapter 44 undermine Chapters 60 *and* 61? A second approach to the false ending might investigate its subversion of the hierarchy of discourse referred to by Belsey (see above). The absurdly brief reduction of Charles and Ernestina's marriage to a paragraph and the fates of the others to a few lines is supposed to be a figment of *Charles's* imagination (327). In other words, the protagonist is given the role of narrator for a chapter or so, but the 'real' narrator does not bother to tell the reader until afterwards. Thus the conventional dominance of the organizing narrative voice is undermined – but how far? Is the reader now to assume that *any* subsequent chapter might emerge from a character's fantasy? The most obvious and comforting answer is 'no', as otherwise the rest of the novel would be impossible to read. Nevertheless, a lingering doubt remains: for instance, to what extent do the closed and open endings satisfy Charles's dreams of regaining Sarah and finding existential freedom respectively? Finally, Chapter 44 might be read as emblematic of *The French Lieutenant's Woman*'s irony: in the unlikely event that the reader has trusted the narrator thus far, Chapter 44 will remove any illusion of credibility, and force the reader to form his or her own interpretation of events. As we cannot trust Fowles's narrator, we are led, in existentialist fashion, to trust ourselves.

DISCUSSION QUESTIONS

1. Fowles's wife Elizabeth dissuaded him from having a single, closed conclusion, with Sarah and Charles reunited. When Fowles wrote the dual ending, he put the closed conclusion last, but his editor Tom Maschler suggested what became the final order, with the open ending last. How important is the dual ending to the novel, and how important is the order of the endings? Would the novel have been improved had they been the other way round, or if only one ending (either closed or open) had been published? In each case, why?

2. Fowles's wife Elizabeth made him delete a comic passage in an early draft, in which the narrator appears as a notorious murderer who escapes from a lunatic asylum in Exeter. Charles looks exactly like him and is detained by the police (Warburton, 2004, 294). Would such a passage have weakened the novel, if allowed to reach the final version? If so, why?

3. How intrusive or not are the appearances of the narrator? Do his attempts to pose as the novelist (for example, in Chapter 13) detract from the main narrative or add to it?

CHAPTER 3

READING THE NOVEL

To read *The French Lieutenant's Woman* is to follow the basic romance plot of the meeting, separation and reunion of Charles and Sarah. It is also to take a long, circuitous journey through Victorian literature, evolutionary science, Marxism, psychoanalysis, poststructuralist literary theory and the discourses of fashion, sexuality and the law. It is reductive to impose any single overarching interpretation on such a diverse text. Instead, as with many novels, probably the best way to begin a critical account of *The French Lieutenant's Woman* is to select chapters that seem appealing for their complexity or ambiguity and work through them carefully. This will involve looking for features of style, literary devices and references to key themes, as well as connections to other parts of the book, other texts, or the cultural context. Out of a close reading of several passages, an overall interpretation can gradually be built up. Each of the critical readings in this chapter, which are set out in separate sections, can be connected with the others, used as a springboard for your own ideas, adapted and, of course, disagreed with. The chapter will conclude with some topics for further discussion.

RELIGION AND NATURE

In Chapter 29, Charles leaves Lyme and journeys through the Undercliff in order to meet Sarah at Carslake's Barn (an abandoned building there), in defiance of his earlier agreement to send Dr Grogan instead, and have Sarah confined to a lunatic asylum. The chapter is an ideal place for the narrator to focus on Charles's relationship to the natural world, and on two of the novel's central ideas, Darwinism and religion. Charles is forced to realize that his Linnaean system for naming and organizing nature, inherited through his scientific training, is completely inadequate when confronted with the vivid, unclassifiable scene before him:

> Charles felt himself walking through the pages of a bestiary, and one of such beauty, such minute distinctness, that every leaf in it, each small bird, each song it uttered, came from a perfect world. He stopped a moment, so struck was he by this sense of an exquisitely particular universe, in which each was appointed, each unique. (233)

Charles can no longer reduce the plants and animals around him to mere instances of genus, phylum and species. They appear as individuals, and in this they are 'perfect'. The particularity of each being before him reflects intelligent design, as each is 'appointed' to be so, as is 'every leaf' (meaning page, as well as plant organ) in the bestiary (or text) of nature: the design, though, is Darwinian rather than divine. Charles perceives the scene as beautiful, but his mood changes when he finds himself astonished by a wren, singing on a branch a few feet away, because it appears to him to be 'the Announcing Angel of evolution: I am what I am, thou shalt not pass my being now' (233). Charles feels that his own existence is mundane when compared to the vivid reality of this unique creature.

The narrator points out that the significance of the individual over the species, and of existence over death, is taken for granted by the modern mind, and 'we cannot imagine' how the message of the wren appears hostile or threatening to Charles (234). This is knowingly overstated, as the narrator is trying to help the reader to imagine just that. The wren's affirmation of its unique existence recalls God's declaration to Moses: 'I am that I am' (Exodus 3.14), and St Paul's statement of the role of God in creating him as an apostle: 'But by the grace of God I am what I am' (1 Corinthians 15.10). So Charles and the reader are confronted with a tiny apostolic bird that declares its presence in the design of evolution with tremendous existential force, announcing the triumph of Darwinian theory with a power that echoes divine revelation. The scene's Bakhtinian dialogue between scientific and religious discourses gives a sense of the power of the dilemma that is overwhelming Charles: 'Fowles's Undercliff acquires a moral charge by its associations with both religious and counter-religious texts' (Aubrey, 1999, 24). Charles sees the Undercliff in both scientific and spiritual terms: he realizes that a 'universal chaos' of particularity lurks beneath his 'pseudo-Linnaean' notions of order and species, but, at the same time, the wren inhabits an Eden from which he is 'excommunicated [. . .] all paradise lost' (234). The allusion to Milton's epic poem of the fall of man is brief, but, earlier on, the narrator provides a more substantial Renaissance reference. He compares Charles to St Eustace (also called St Hubert) in Antonio Pisanello's 1436 painting *The Vision of St Eustace*, in which the saint, while travelling in the forest, suddenly finds himself 'shocked' by a secret he had not known until that moment: 'the universal parity of existence' (233). The point the narrator derives from Pisanello is that the saint, through his confrontation with nature, is confronted by divine creativity (symbolized in the painting by a stag with a crucifix in its antlers), in which he has previously placed an abstract faith, but which now staggers him with the force of its directly felt reality. St Hubert's faith is in Christianity and Charles believes in evolution, but the shock of the confrontation is the same, creating 'a moment of epiphany' (Warburton, 1999, 116).

There is another epiphany to follow, this time caused by Sarah. When Charles arrives at the barn, she is not to be seen: Charles is afraid he will find a corpse. Sarah's absence is typical of her elusiveness. She remains mysterious throughout the novel: 'she is finally unknowable; and her resistance to interpretation is connected [. . .] with her capacity to educate' (Conradi, 1982, 64). She is linked to nature, ambiguity and mystery. Her name, Woodruff, means 'bramble bush', and she is associated with the Undercliff, whose wildness is one of 'the physical correlatives of her psychic landscape and emotional weather' (Ross, 1999, 187). Sorrow wells out of her face 'as purely, naturally and unstoppably as water out of a woodland spring' (*FLW*, 16) but the source of that sorrow remains opaque: Grogan can only classify it as 'obscure melancholia' (151). Suzanne Ross points out that although critics have seen Sarah's mysteriousness as an objectification of her femininity, in which her silence is associated with her gender, so that she becomes 'as a woman, absent and voiceless' (Ross, 1999, 181), it could equally be seen as part of Fowles's *critique* of such objectification, whereby 'Sarah's actions open up to reinterpretation and revision the story of the [patriarchal] bond linking women more closely to nonhuman nature' (190). Thus Sarah's association with mystery and with nature might be read in two opposed ways: as a means of subtly, perhaps unintentionally, imprinting a reactionary view of her femininity on the reader, or as a device to make *The French Lieutenant's Woman* suggest the feminist message that male interpretations of women are inadequate. In either case, Sarah remains a fascinating figure, exemplifying Fowles's theory that unexplained mystery energizes a story, just as it drives the human urge to comprehend the universe. Fowles believes that 'gaps in understanding and narrative' are a very important part of our relationship to fiction and the natural world:

> ambiguity is a very important part of the experience [of reading]. That's why I like nature. There's so much of it we just cannot understand. (*Con*, 155)

In Chapter 31, when Sarah finally appears at the barn, Charles is confronted with *her* mystery, in a deliberate echo of his encounter with unclassifiable nature in the wood. 'There was a wildness about her' (240), which Charles realizes is not the wildness of hysteria but the same wildness he associated with the wren. If the bird announced evolution with biblical force, so Sarah announces existentialism with her physical presence. Charles becomes detached from such Victorian notions as duty and propriety, and lets his personal impulses guide him. The chapter ends with Charles and Sarah's first kiss, after 'the moment overcame the age' (243). Thus the plot advances, and the characters develop, as the protagonists' affection becomes openly sexual. The novel's exposition of ideas also progresses, as the moment of their kiss symbolizes the triumph of evolving existentialist chaos over static Victorian order.

Charles's fear that he will see a dead woman at the barn stems from his inherited patriarchal mind-set that sees the world as 'metaphorically "dead"', because fixed and knowable (Warburton, 1999, 118). Charles's expectation of a corpse is framed by a Gothic simile, as Sarah's bonnet 'hung like an ominously slaked vampire over what he could not yet see' (*FLW*, 235). This resembles the sex scene in the hotel, when Charles, sounding like the narrator of a Victorian sensation novel, believes that Sarah has lied to him about her virginity for the purpose of 'Blackmail! To put him totally in her power!' (341). In each case, an allusion to popular Victorian plots is introduced when Charles is experiencing anti-existentialist fear. Conventional emotion brings references to conventional literature: the protagonists' lives are echoed by intertextual allusion. However, as Eileen Warburton has argued, when the rising of the living woman integrates Charles with the world around him, he is granted what Fowles has called 'Whole sight' (*DM*, 7), a true vision of himself and his situation: 'For a brief moment, he is embraced, enfolded, and sees clearly and "whole"' (Warburton, 1999, 118).

INTERTEXTUALITY AND POWER

The French Lieutenant's Woman is a historical novel that exposes history as a problem, rather than a source of truth. It is a practical demonstration of an issue faced not only by historians looking back at the past, but also by those living through any age: of how to arrive at the truth, or a working interpretation of it, when ideologies in dialogue with one another compete for priority. One such struggle occurs within Charles, when he tries to work out Sarah's mental state. Sarah's first look at Charles on the Cobb is sufficient to convince him that she is not insane: 'above all, [there was] no sign of madness' in her face (16). His assessment of her basic sanity, coming so early, is later challenged by Grogan. The result of this challenge is a power struggle within

Charles, in which quotations from competing texts represent the discourses of romantic love and existential freedom versus those of science and Victorian propriety. At Carslake's Barn, one main source is quoted:

> 'My dear Miss Woodruff, pray control yourself. I –'
> 'I cannot.'
> The words were barely audible, but they silenced Charles. He tried to tell himself that she meant she could not control her gratitude for his charity . . . he tried, he tried. But there came on him a fleeting memory of Catullus: 'Whenever I see you, sound fails, my tongue falters, thin fire steals through my limbs, an inner roar, and darkness shrouds my ears and eyes.' Catullus was translating Sappho here; and the Sapphic remains the best clinical description of love in European medicine. (242: ellipsis in original)

Charles uses classical sources. He cites the ancient Roman poet Catullus's translation of the ancient Greek poetess Sappho to describe what he believes are Sarah's emotions; according to the narrator, Charles is showing symptoms of the same feelings, although he denies them (242). Despite the historical distance between Sappho and the protagonists, the narrator does not suggest that the citation is anachronistic; instead, he claims, with tongue partly in cheek, that Sappho's account of these symptoms is still a perfect 'clinical description'.

Katherine Tarbox believes that the novel is implying that love transcends history: 'The feeling [of love] is constant, as shown by Charles's hurtling back through ages to be joined in emotion to Sappho' (Tarbox, 1989, 79). However, she qualifies her point by adding 'even though Charles's tortured behaviour seems a parody of love' (79). This somewhat undermines Tarbox's argument, because it implies that the meaning of love may change radically over time. Is Charles experiencing the same emotion as Sappho, or is he forced to parody this emotion (meaning, in this case, imitate it badly) because of his historical context, which makes his feelings dangerous and blameworthy? Charles is not merely in love; he is in love with a fallen woman and a social inferior, a potentially disastrous combination. Moreover, Sappho's words are to be read in the 'clinical' context of 'European medicine'. The narrator's reference to medicine is more than just a playful irony: it suggests that the symptoms described by Sappho may be used as evidence towards a diagnosis of pathological behaviour. Sarah's 'I cannot', meaning 'I cannot deny myself', creates an echo of Ernestina's 'I must not' (34), which means the exact opposite. Ernestina's phrase places her safely within Victorian sexual conventions, but Sarah's places her – and Charles – dangerously outside them. Grogan diagnoses Sarah as pathological when, as a way of warning Charles away from her, he declares that her behaviour is the result of 'a deranged mind' (217). So Charles and Sarah may be experiencing similar emotions to those of Sappho, but their historical context utterly transforms the *significance* of these emotions. Charles's love is also thoroughly historicized by means of the quotation itself. He is citing a classical poem to describe amorous emotion, or the symptoms of insanity, the way only a man of his education, and therefore his social class, could have done in 1867. Charles cannot escape the texts he has read, the social system permitting them to be read together, and the Victorian ideology behind that system.

Charles is not describing Sarah's feelings, because he does not know them. Instead, he is using Sappho to construct his own interpretation of what they *may* be, based on Sarah's appearance, words and actions. By co-opting the lyric of a pre-Christian woman, the nineteenth-century man is casting Sarah in a certain mould, creating an image of Sarah-as-lover. Similarly, the quotation of the poem has a constitutive effect on Charles himself, by developing his nascent existentialist identity. His feeling of abandon, derived from Sappho, permits him to undertake certain actions, such as kissing Sarah, and having sexual intercourse with her in the hotel room. The later scene echoes that of the barn: Sappho's imagery of fire returns, and is used by the narrator to describe Charles's justification for his behaviour. He feels the need 'to possess her, to melt into her, to burn, to burn, to burn to ashes on that body and in those eyes [. . .] Those same mysterious syncopal symptoms as in the barn swept over him' (334–5).

Sarah, and particularly her eyes, have been consistently associated with fire; 'Sarah was all flame. Her eyes were all flame' (242). By the time of the tryst at Exeter, Charles has consciously entered the Sapphic discourse, and constitutes himself as the object turned to ashes by love's incendiary power.

Charles's need to 'melt into' Sarah, and the consequent sex act between them is the final outcome of a power struggle between propriety and love. From early on, Charles has been aware that meeting Sarah alone in the Undercliff represents a transgression of social and sexual morality: 'He knew he was about to engage in the forbidden' (144). It is only at the barn, though, after several such meetings, that he overcomes his inhibitions, and expresses his affection physically. The discourses of propriety, which reinforce Charles's self-restraint, include those of 'the doctors' (242) who would characterize Sarah as a hysteric. The first of these doctors is Grogan, present in the flesh, and the second Karl Matthaei, present in textual form as the writer of *Observations Médico-psychologiques*, a book that Grogan shows to Charles. Matthaei explains that hysteria is 'the assumption [. . .] of symptoms of disease or disability in order to gain the attention and sympathy of others' (226).

Charles's inner struggle between love and duty has an intertextual basis as much as an emotional one. As well as being derived from Sappho, it represents a development of the rarefied struggles between courtly love and fealty experienced by the 'parfit knights and *preux chevaliers* of the Middle Ages' (285). Sarah, too, for all her proto-existentialism, may be in a similar position, in that her feelings have a basis in literature: 'Without realizing it she judged people as much by the standards of Walter Scott and Jane Austen as by any empirically arrived at' (58). To textualize the emotions of the protagonists is not to force them out of history or to make them unaffected by social context. On the contrary, *The French Lieutenant's Woman* shows how an emotion quoted from a literary source may have its significance completely altered by the historical circumstances of the character quoting it. In the hotel room, when Charles experiences post-coital regret, he feels that his emotions cannot exist for himself and his beloved alone, but are enacted before an imaginary audience of judgemental peers: 'guilt crept, crept through his nerves and veins. In the distant shadows Ernestina stood and stared mournfully at him. Mr Freeman struck him across the face' (338). To suggest Charles's change of attitude, the narrator adapts Sappho's language of passion to suggest shame and culpability: instead of 'thin fire' stealing through his limbs, Charles feels guilt creeping through his body. Thus the protagonists' emotions, although taken from the novel's literary sources, are affected by the force of circumstance, and cannot transcend time or place.

Neither Sappho's lyric nor Matthaei's medical text is left unmodified by *The French Lieutenant's Woman*. Each quotation is a reformulation of the source, in which it serves a new purpose. The novel treats Matthaei's and Sappho's texts neither as objects of mockery nor as documents to be revered, but incorporates them into its narrative, reworking them even when it quotes them verbatim. Matthaei's text, for instance, is cited without interruption for over two pages. Matthaei lends to his testimony all the force of his training and accumulated experience, to support his thesis that young women can fake illness to get what they want:

> If I glance back over my long career as a doctor, I recall many incidents of which girls have been the heroines, although their participation seemed for long impossible [. . .] After such examples, which it would be easy to extend, who would say that it is impossible for a girl, in order to attain a desired end, to inflict pain upon herself? (226–9)

Grogan intends Sarah to be one of Matthaei's 'girls' and Charles does not miss the hint. However, Matthaei's rhetoric does not, in the end, change Charles's love for her. Although Charles is at first shocked, he re-reads the text and discovers that Sarah fits the picture of a hysteric less well than Grogan supposes:

> He tried to recollect her face, things she had said, the expression in her eyes as she had said them; but he could not grasp her. Yet it came to him that he knew her better, perhaps, than any other human being did. (230)

Charles is left with only fragments of Sarah; and yet, this incomplete apprehension is, he believes, knowledge. Indeed, he thinks that he may know her better than anyone else does. Matthaei's text, by contrast, does not allow Charles to know Sarah. Although Sarah admits that she effectively arranged her own dismissal from Mrs Poulteney's house (243) and that she lied to Charles over Varguennes (341), her spontaneous admission of her own deceit makes her very different from any of the women described by Matthaei, who had all 'waited to be caught before confession' (242). By defying 'the doctors', Charles is placing himself beyond the pale of Victorian convention, which would marginalize Sarah. Matthaei's text, because of its sheer dead weight, suggested by the length of the quotation, becomes a metonym for this convention. This, in itself, represents an appropriation of the source: when first written, Matthaei's words were intended not to reinforce convention, but to subvert it. They were designed to aid the defence of Emile de La Roncière (an alleged attempted rapist, tried in 1835, whose supposed victim was, in Matthaei's view, experiencing a hysterical fantasy). Matthaei's aim was to help La Roncière's society to break free of its own 'psychological ignorance' (226). This is part of the novel's complex historical irony: texts such as those of Matthaei and Sappho are taken out of their original contexts and manipulated according to the needs of the present.

INTERTEXTUALITY AND STRUCTURE

Sometimes, *The French Lieutenant's Woman* uses a subtler form of intertextual reference, which avoids direct quotation, but nevertheless establishes an ironic link with a source through playful imitation. For example, on returning to his inn after his sexual encounter with Sarah, Charles goes upstairs, bathes, and washes the bloodstains (caused by the breaking of Sarah's hymen) off his clothes: 'Some fifteen minutes later you might have seen Charles stark naked and engaged in an unaccustomed occupation: that of laundering' (355). He leaves his clothes over the side of the bath, to conceal the fact that he has been washing them. This is a direct allusion to an incident in Thomas Hardy's novel

The Well-Beloved (first published in 1892), discussed by Fowles in his essay 'Hardy and the Hag':

> the strange near-fetishist scene, the most overtly erotic in the book, when Pierston dries Marcia's wet clothes at the inn, manipulating the veils while the baggageless dancer stands naked in his imagination, if not his sight, upstairs. (*W*, 172)

Pierston and Marcia are caught in the rain, like Charles; Charles washes his own clothes, whereas Pierston dries his own, then dismisses the night porter so he can dry Marcia's also (Hardy, 1964, 27). In *The French Lieutenant's Woman*'s version, the naked person is also upstairs at the inn; but this time, it is the man who is naked, and he is cleaning the woman's blood off his clothes. The scene takes place after intercourse rather than in anticipation of it, and the man is trying to remove the sign of his guilt. This is part of *The French Lieutenant's Woman*'s affectionate but sceptical re-enactment of Hardy's eroticism. It also exposes the limitations of readings which claim that 'Fowles's book is quite overtly a fantasy of dominance and submission in which [Sarah] is made both sexual and threatening' (Woodcock, 1984, 103). In fact, Charles ends up in a position of submission, but only because he is performing an action normally given to a servant, by furtively washing the clothes: to interpret this as merely the expression of a fetishist 'fantasy' seems somewhat misguided. Instead, it is an imitation of an earlier version of such a fantasy, achieved by re-enacting the scene from Hardy.

The French Lieutenant's Woman's parodies of its Victorian sources help to inform the plot, which is built on a fluctuating combination of similarity to and difference from the romance narratives of the nineteenth century. Particular characters, themes and actions copy their Victorian ancestors but also diverge from them either blatantly or subtly. This can be seen, for instance, when the novel alludes to a stereotypical Victorian literary figure: the institutionalized female. Grogan's proposal to confine Sarah to an asylum echoes many mid-Victorian sensation novels – for instance, Wilkie Collins's *The Woman in White* (1860) and Mary Elizabeth Braddon's *Lady Audley's Secret*

(1862). In the former, Laura Fairlie, although sane, is confined to a madhouse. In the latter, the confined protagonist is an arsonist and murderess who confesses her crimes, but only when she has been caught. Lady Audley is one of the sources, other than Matthaei, for the narrator's remarks about female hysterics: 'The distinguished young ladies who had gone in for house-burning' and who had only owned up when discovered (242). This is also a reference to a canonical text, Charlotte Brontë's *Jane Eyre*, first published in 1847, in which Bertha Mason, who has been deemed insane, is confined to Rochester's attic then escapes to burn down his mansion.

The French Lieutenant's Woman alludes to the institutionalized woman trope by appearing to reject it, as Charles helps Sarah to flee to London. However, Sarah does not completely escape institutionalization, because the trope is cited again, in modified form, at the time of her final meeting with Charles, when she is confined to the Rossetti household. Sarah is highly regarded there, as a model and muse, but, at the same time, her role as Rossetti's assistant can be read as a marginal one. Her marginalization has been foregrounded by feminist readers: Sarah plays 'the role of the passive female object inspiring or enabling a male act of artistic creation' (Kadish, 1997, 84). Pamela Cooper sees it as typical of Fowles's fictions, which deprive their heroines of creativity and language even while seeming to confer power and significance upon them: 'in order to preserve the inarticulate essence of Sarah [. . .] the novel deprives her of her narratorial role and recasts her as muse and model to artists' (Cooper, 1991, 122).

When Sarah first appears to Charles in Rossetti's house, she is dressed 'in the full uniform of the New Woman' (*FLW*, 423), with a pink-and-white striped blouse, gilt star clasp and blue skirt. The patterns and colours echo those of the Stars and Stripes, the flag of the United States, seen by the narrator as the crucible of women's liberation (414). Nevertheless, Sarah is constrained by her role within the bohemian household at 16 Cheyne Walk. Here, *The French Lieutenant's Woman* is compromising its own portrayal of its heroine as an existentialist. After following the narrator's gloss on Matthew Arnold's *Notebooks* and '*acting what* [she] *knows'* (440; emphasis in original) for most of the novel, Sarah seems to retreat from this independence, and to become a vehicle for male art, and also part of history, in the sense of the documented past. Moreover, she is affected by the power relations that formed that past. It is the reader, aware of the canonical importance of the Pre-Raphaelites, who will inevitably confine Sarah within a *cultural* institution. This process has been continued by critics, who have quite rightly seen a strong parallel between Sarah and Rossetti's wife and model, Lizzie Siddal. Sarah has the same 'red-gold' hair and, in at least one reader's view, represents 'a truly uncanny presentation' of Siddal (Warburton, 1999, 134 n.).

The claim that Sarah is silenced by intertextuality and history gains ground when she says 'I am not to be understood even by myself' (431). Cooper uses this to argue that her silence is absolutely necessary to the novel. Any self-comprehension on her part 'would destroy that innocence which stands for the purity of the text. It would categorically ally her [. . .] to the destructive fragmentations – the sheer *knowingness* – of post-modernism' (Cooper, 1991, 138; emphasis in original). Sarah certainly claims not to know herself, and much of her behaviour would confirm this. Nevertheless, the novel's intertextuality militates against any 'innocence which stands for the purity of the text'. During its construction of its heroine, the novel shows how it knows itself – and Sarah – to be *im*pure, as both text and character are built out of modified fragments of sources such as Hardy, Matthaei, Rossetti, Braddon, Sappho, and so on.

This has implications for the novel's gender politics. If Sarah and Charles's relationship is built out of a number of allusions, how might this affect a feminist reading? Does the novel's repeated imitation of female roles taken from Victorian literature (Sarah as governess seeking independence, but also as fallen woman and potential asylum inmate; Ernestina as spoilt rich girl, then betrayed fiancée), and eventual placing of Sarah within the Rossetti household, simply reflect the condition of women in the male-dominated world of art and literature, or attempt to advance that condition, or form yet another variation on a long-standing patriarchal fantasy of women as passionate, dangerous beings associated with untamed nature, who benefit most from some sort of institutional control? To follow this up, it is necessary to consider the novel's constructions of gender and sexuality.

THE PRODUCTION OF SEXUALITY

James Acheson has rightly claimed that one reason Fowles's novels have sold so widely is that 'sex figures prominently in all of them' (Acheson, 1998, 1); he reads *The French Lieutenant's Woman* as an exposure of Victorian sexual hypocrisy (2). The novel goes further than this, though, by questioning the cultural myths that link gender, sexuality and society in our own time as well as in the nineteenth century. For example, in Chapter 60, when Sarah appears to refuse his offer of marriage, Charles feels that 'Some terrible perversion of human sexual destiny had begun' (433). When he connects sexuality and destiny, Charles shows that he is influenced by the ideology that shapes people's lives, especially those of women, in terms of marriage and reproduction. Since the 1990s, queer theory has referred to this cultural myth as 'heteronarrative' (e.g. Roof, 1996, 172–9). *The French Lieutenant's Woman* anticipates queer theory's interrogation of heteronarrative when it plays games with the gender destinies of its protagonists. In fact, the novel refuses to make them destinies at all, by leaving them indeterminate. The three endings give Charles very different sexual futures: as married to Ernestina; as reunited with Sarah; and as an existentially free bachelor. Thus the text does more than expose Victorian hypocrisy: it manipulates the dominant narrative of sexual norms that determines the fate not only of Victorians but also of people in the twentieth century and beyond, depending on their gender, social status and degree of existential freedom.

To illustrate the importance of the novel's interrogation of Victorian *and* contemporary myths of gender and sexuality, it is worth looking closely at a passage where the narrator not only offers his own judgement of the sexuality of one of the characters and the mores of Victorian age she inhabits, but also reveals much about his own character and historical background. The scene shows how the novel builds up a picture of Victorian sexuality – or, rather, a modern image of it. This image is not objective, but is problematic precisely *because* it is modern.

> [Ernestina] had evolved a kind of private commandment – those inaudible words were simply 'I must not' – whenever the physical female implications of her body, sexual, menstrual, parturitional, tried to force an entry into her consciousness. But though one may keep the wolves from one's door, they still howl out there in the darkness. Ernestina wanted a husband, wanted Charles to be that husband, wanted children; but the payment she vaguely divined she would have to make for them seemed excessive.
>
> She sometimes wondered why God had permitted such a bestial version of Duty to spoil such an innocent longing. Most women of her period felt the same; so did most men; and it is no wonder that duty has become such a key concept in our understanding of the Victorian age – or for that matter, such a wet blanket in our own.* [. . .]
>
> *The stanzas from *In Memoriam* I have quoted at the begin- ning of this chapter are very relevant here [. . .] To claim that love can only be Satyr-shaped if there is no immortality of the soul is clearly a panic flight from Freud. Heaven for the Victorians was very largely heaven because the body was left behind – along with the Id. (34–5)

The narrator explores the implications of 'I must not', Ernestina's personal litany of self-denial. Sounding like a text- book, he introduces duty as a 'key concept', and adds a footnote that helpfully links Ernestina's self-censorship to the chapter's epigraph from Tennyson's *In Memoriam*. This consists of two stanzas in which Tennyson puts the case for an afterlife, by claim- ing that if death were final, then love would only be meaningful in its 'coarsest Satyr-shape', i.e. as the expression of sexual desire, an urge to cheat death through reproduction (31). The narrator adds his own Freudian reading of Tennyson's poem as a denial of the body, and connects this to the Victorian dichotomy of body and soul, in which the former was allegedly considered bestial and best left behind on death. In a rapid and daring move from the particular to the general, the narrator shifts the story's focus from one woman's expression of self-denial to the ideology of a whole historical period, followed by a thumbnail sketch of the psychoanalytical perspective of a later period upon it.

Given the virtuosity and erudition of this performance, it seems difficult to do other than absorb what the narrator says and take it on trust. Some of his statements seem intuitively true: if one accepts the twentieth-century stereotype of the Victorian age as sexually repressed, then his points about duty and the Victorian flight from Freud appear to be accurate. His use of Freud, though, strikes a historically false note. Freud was born in 1856, and *The Interpretation of Dreams* was first published in German in 1900; his work was only translated into English in the following decades, and thus had no impact on Victorian culture. In a similar instance, the narrator draws irony from the fact that although Karl Marx published the first volume of *Capital* in the year the novel is set, 1867, and wrote the work in England, he was totally unknown to most British Victorians (this is explored further later in this chapter). Just as they were unperturbed by Marxism, how can the Victorians have fled from an unconscious that did not yet exist? The answer seems to be that when he refers to 'Freud', what the narrator actually means is a reality Freud *described*, but which was supposedly consistent through history and true before it was written down: a reality of a mind divided between an ego, which forces unacceptable thoughts into the unconscious through repression, and an id, which stores the repressed thoughts, only to return them to consciousness in the form of neuroses and night-mares. By this reading, the narrator does not refer to Freud's actual work, but the uncomfortable, universal truths about the mind it unearthed. However, it is equally possible to argue that Freud did not describe but *created* a truth about the mind: an idea suited to the twentieth century, driven by modern circumstances, which could be used to *interpret* the present and the past rather than state objective truths about either. Michel Foucault, for instance, points out the significance of the historical conditions under which psychoanalysis emerged, and its role as a reaction to nineteenth-century sexual science. Freud's theories 'sought to free [the sexual instinct] from its ties with heredity, and hence from eugenics and the various racisms' that were prevalent at the end of the Victorian period and beyond (Foucault, 1990, 119).

A subtle warning to the reader is sounded when Fowles's narrator says duty is important not to the Victorians as such, but to 'our understanding' of them: it is implied that duty matters as much to the twentieth century as a negative term, a means of distancing itself from the past, as it ever did to the Victorians as a moral imperative. Duty is elsewhere glossed as 'agreeable conformity to the epoch's current' (*FLW*, 54): by this definition, it is dutiful in the modern era to look down on the Victorians as conformist and repressed. There is also the narrator's footnote: why is Tennyson's statement about love and death '*clearly* a *panic* flight from Freud' (emphasis added)? The narrator seems replete with judgemental historical hindsight. Later on, he states that Victorian hysteria was 'caused, *as we now know*, by sexual repression' (226: emphasis added). The reader can interpret this as the truth about the Victorian age, or as merely a late twentieth-century interpretation of that age, moulded by the later period's somewhat narcissistic image of itself as cleverer, less repressed, more liberated – overall, more knowing.

Foucault has argued that the Victorian age was not in fact characterized by repression, but by a constant flow of discourse about sexuality, in which new permissions and prohibitions, new categories of the normal and perverse, and new confessions of sexual sin were being created all the time by means of medicine, science, religion, pornography, popular culture, and so on: 'Rather than a massive censorship [. . .] what was involved was a regulated and polymorphous incitement to discourse' (Foucault, 1990, 34). Ernestina's spoken recognition of her sexuality through 'I must not', and the brief vision of naked limbs that inspires it (34), are as typically Victorian as her self-denial. Ernestina, in fact, produces sexual discourse even as she censors her speech. Ernestina has a 'profound ignorance' of sex and to her it is surrounded by an 'aura of pain and brutality' which denies the gentleness and 'discreetness of permitted caress' she sees in Charles (34); but what is happening here is that she is finding ways of expressing her relationship to her sexuality. In

Foucault's sense, she is *creating* her own sexuality by making it something distant and frightening that can nevertheless be imagined and covertly acknowledged.

The narrator makes his opinions on Victorian sexuality clearest in Chapter 35. The first two pages outline Victorian hypocrisy, giving such examples as: the hiding of the female body from view, yet the judging of any sculptor by his ability to carve naked women; the lack of any sensuality beyond a kiss in any literary novel, set against the vast output of pornography; and the fact that women were not supposed to have orgasms, 'yet every prostitute was taught to simulate them' (259).

> [The Victorians] were quite as highly sexed as our own century – and, in spite of the fact that *we* have sex thrown at us night and day (as the Victorians had religion), far more preoccupied with it than we really are. [. . .] The Victorians chose to be serious about something we treat rather lightly, and the way they expressed their seriousness was not to *talk openly* about sex, just as part of our way is the very reverse. But these 'ways' of being serious are mere conventions. The fact behind them remains constant. (259–60: emphasis in original)

Unlike Foucault, the narrator characterizes the Victorian period as governed by 'a convention of suppression, repression and silence' (261), and argues that such conventions governing sexuality are ways of dealing with a universal constant, rather than of producing sexuality, as Foucault would have it, in the form of discourse. He goes so far as to claim that sexual discourse is inimical to sexual pleasure: the twentieth century is 'the more Victorian – in the derogatory sense of the word' (261), since it has destroyed much of the enjoyment and mystery of sexuality by bringing it into the open.

Critics are divided on how to deal with statements like this. M. Keith Booker believes that 'This rather romantic argument is highly suspect' (Booker, 1991, 194). Booker is suspicious not about Fowles, but about the argument itself as offered by the narrator. He suggests that the novel is playing a highly sophisticated game, and is ironically questioning both Victorian and contemporary attitudes towards sexuality, by 'calling into question the assumption that our modern treatment of sexuality is superior to that of the Victorians (and vice versa)' (194). Peter Conradi comes close to Booker's position, but sees the text's game as one of seduction and betrayal of the reader: the novel works by 'giving a seductive action of sexual compulsion and moral emancipation, but properly interrupting this [. . .] with stern and bracing rebukes to our credulity' (Conradi, 1982, 67) in which we are warned not to believe the romance plot even as we enjoy reading it. Michael Mason disagrees. Unlike Booker and Conradi, he sees the text's appearance of sophistication as superficial, and claims that the author is misguided: 'the implication Fowles sees here, that Victorian women were not thought to enjoy sex, cannot be drawn'. He asserts that Fowles 'cannot bear to seem ignorant', and that his text shows a 'ridiculously bad' grasp of Victorian history (Mason, 1981, 1391). Bruce Woodcock also censures Fowles, but because of his alleged patriarchal attitude, which stems from male anxieties about 1960s feminism: Fowles's narrator offers 'repeated nostalgia for the romance and mystery of the days when men were men and women were women. [. . .] He envies the Victorians for their [sexual] reserve' (Woodcock, 1984, 91).

I have already argued, against the views of Woodcock and Mason, that the novel can be read as challenging heteronarrative assumptions, that it exposes the production of sexuality in the Victorian period even when the characters attempt to deny their sexual impulses, and that the narrator's sense of his own modern hindsight can be read as an ironic exposure of twentieth-century complacency. This applies regardless of Fowles's intent, which may have been simply a storyteller's wish to seduce the reader, as Conradi argues, or a working out of his own masculine anxieties about the women's movement, as Woodcock believes. The narrator may sound patriarchal and even make historical errors, as Mason claims, but the novel offers a dynamic, multifaceted picture of Victorian sexuality. For instance, Sam and Mary have far less trouble than Charles and Sarah in admitting their sexual attraction for one another, and acting upon their desires, because they come from a lower social stratum.

Among the rural working class, pre-marital sex '*was the rule, not the exception*' (262; emphasis in original). In fact, they conceive their first child (a daughter, like Charles and Sarah's Lalage) at Carslake's Barn (401). A triangulation of Ernestina's vocal denial of her own erotic visions with Charles and Sarah's release from repression at Carslake's Barn and the more open sexuality of Sam and Mary would suggest that Victorian sexual roles were many, and varied according to social and financial status as well as gender and the age and expectations of the individual. The novel suggests too much about the complex, multiform production of sexuality in the nineteenth century to allow generalizations about 'the Victorians' – including those made by the narrator – to be given too much weight.

MARXISM AND SOCIAL CLASS

As a parable of the confrontation between existential freedom and conventional conformity, *The French Lieutenant's Woman* might seem to celebrate the individual over the mass. However, set against this is the epigraph that precedes the novel (though not in every edition), 'Every emancipation is a restoration of the human world and of human relationships to man himself' (Marx, 1975, 234, cited in *FLW*, n. p.). This statement is taken from *Zur Judenfrage* (*On the Jewish Question*), the work of Karl Marx (1818–83), the German philosopher whose work created modern communism. Marx's concern was not with an antisocial, individualistic notion of freedom, but with emancipation, which can be achieved only with reference to the human subject's relations to others, and its existence as a species-being: 'Only when real, individual man [. . .] has become a *species-being* in his empirical life [. . .] will human emancipation be completed' (Marx, 1975, 234: emphasis in original). Simon Loveday claims that the epigraph

> succinctly prefigures [the novel's] reconciliation of freedom and responsibility by suggesting that every one of us carries some responsibility for the emancipation, the releasing into freedom, of the whole human race. (Loveday, 1985, 74)

As Loveday implies, the plot of *The French Lieutenant's Woman* is based on the efforts of its protagonists to achieve a form of emancipation. However, despite the epigraph, the text does not reconcile individual freedom with social responsibility, or imply that a person can only achieve emancipation through becoming a '*species-being*' in Marxist fashion. Charles and Sarah are given freedom in the final ending (Chapter 61), but only through the permanent severing of their bond, and the cessation of their relationship. Ironically, it is in the closed ending (Chapter 60), which does offer a restoration of this relationship, through the protagonists' acceptance of their dual responsibility for their child, that their emancipation is denied, and existential freedom is abandoned in favour of conformity. In this version of events, the 'intervening god' is *not* that of Chapter 61, 'life as we have [. . .] made it ourselves, life as Marx defined it – *the actions of men* (and of women) *in pursuit of their ends*' (445: emphasis in original). Here, God is close to a stereotypical Victorian patriarch. Sarah's mysterious behaviour is not her means of freeing Charles, but of expressing her submission to the divine will: 'it had been in God's hands, in His forgiveness of their sins' (438). In neither ending does the 'reconciliation' of freedom and responsibility desired by Loveday occur.

Thus the novel is not simply paraphrasing Marx's notion of the free but socially responsible species-being. Instead, it is playing a series of variations on the Marx epigraph, by offering the protagonists different degrees of personal emancipation and social responsibility in Chapters 60 and 61, and the false ending of Chapter 44 where Charles marries Ernestina. Peter Conradi claims that *The French Lieutenant's Woman*'s narrative voice 'exhibits an earnest grasp of the efficacy of epigraphs' (Conradi, 1982, 69), meaning that the novel reproduces, with irony, a conventional Victorian deployment of epigraphs as a means of informing and instructing the reader through highlighting the content and moral tone of each chapter. Conradi's reading is appropriate to some of the other epigraphs (see below, where those from Arnold and Darwin are discussed), but the quotation from Marx which prefaces the novel is remodelled on existentialist lines. *Zur Judenfrage* is cited in order to foreground the fundamental *tension* between individual freedom and social responsibility which the novel explores but does not resolve. David W. Landrum argues that

> The meta-narrative of Marxism is affirmed in its recognition of the need for emancipation and restoration; but it is also subverted in relation to the substance and nature of the emancipations required to truly restore human relationships. (Landrum, 1996, 103)

The French Lieutenant's Woman incorporates Marxism in order to question it, as Landrum suggests, but the novel's project is not so much to subvert Marx's ideas of emancipation as to open up a dialogue between self-responsibility and responsibility to the social body. The sides of this dialogue are exemplified by the fates of Charles and Sarah in the two endings, in which they have the choice to fit into the Victorian template of the family or remain single and free.

The novel incorporates Marx into the world of the story. In doing so, it raises the issue of the twentieth century's own construction of Marx, and its exploitation of his work. Marx is not named, but alluded to indirectly as the 'German Jew' working in the British Museum while the action of the novel takes place in Lyme (18). The narrator's ethnic identification of Marx places him as an exile, both by his Jewishness and by the fact that he is a German living in Britain: to this extent, he appears constituted by history and by his surroundings. However, Marx's work

> was to bear [. . .] bright red fruit. Had you described that fruit, or the subsequent effects of its later indiscriminate consumption, Charles would almost certainly not have believed you – and even though, in only six months from this March of 1867, the first volume of *Kapital* was to appear in Hamburg. (18)

The narrator places Marx's work as a historical event which would in turn cause others. Marx, it seems, is a 'world-historical individual' in the sense coined by the German idealist philosopher G. W. F. Hegel (1770–1831), an important precursor of

Marx. Such individuals are not constituted by the society around them; instead, they constitute it, producing new historical conditions. They appear to be somehow self-fashioned and mythical:

> They may be called Heroes, inasmuch as they have derived their purposes and their vocation, not from the calm, regular course of things, sanctioned by the existing order; but from a concealed fount – one which has not attained to phenomenal, present existence [. . .] They are men, therefore, who appear to draw the impulse of their life from themselves; and whose deeds have produced a condition of things and a complex of historical relations which appear to be only *their* interest, and *their* work. (Hegel, 1956, 30: emphases in original)

The Marx of *The French Lieutenant's Woman*, though, is hardly a hero. In terms of the intellectual *content* of his work, he does appear self-constituted in the Hegelian manner; however, the political *effect* of that work is seen, in Fowles's novel, as produced by the future, which creates Marx anew according to its own needs. The narrator is busy producing him along with his twentieth-century peers. To describe the effect of Marx's work on the twentieth century, the narrator uses an organic metaphor with both biblical and commercial connotations: his texts produce dangerous fruit which is later indiscriminately consumed. Marx's texts are configured simultaneously as natural growths, symbols of sin, and reified objects of consumption. It appears that Marx is, despite his atheism, an almost Satanic figure and, despite his anti-capitalism, is paradoxically both the producer of twentieth-century society and its product.

To further illustrate the role of Marxism in the novel, we can refer to Chapter 57, which involves the working-class male protagonist, Charles's former servant Sam, who now finds himself part of the business 'empire' (276) of the nouveau-riche Mr Freeman. By February 1869, nearly two years after Charles's arrival in Lyme at the start of the novel, the ironically named arch-plutocrat Freeman is now Sam's employer, having rewarded him for information about Charles's 'guilty secrets' (402). One day, Sam arrives at work at 5 a.m. especially to arrange a set of gentleman's collars to spell 'FREEMAN'S FOR CHOICE' in the window of the London store (404). Mr Freeman likes this so much that he gives Sam a 10 per cent pay rise. Sam has other rises after this, and knows himself to be invaluable: we are told that Sam is now on 32 shillings and sixpence (£1.62½) a week, his house costs £19 a year to rent, and that they pay their servant-girl £6 a year. The narrator's precision about money here shows, in Marxist fashion, how the superstructure of Sam and Mary's family life is founded upon an economic base. Sam still has ambitions to set up in the haberdashery business on his own, but Mary wisely keeps these ambitions in check.

Sam and Mary form a working-class version of Sarah and Charles, except that their ambition to be independent is focused in a materialist rather than existentialist direction. Ironically, as they enter the lower-middle class, Sam and Mary are emancipated by 'the oppressive system that economically exploited them' (Landrum, 1996, 109). Sarah, like Mary, is a servant, and from rural stock, and Sam replaces Charles as a beneficiary, in his own modest way, of the Freeman fortune. The novel sets Sam and Mary up as a relatively happy couple, with one ending to show this, in contrast to the ambiguous dual ending permitted their existentialist cousins Charles and Sarah. We might infer that *The French Lieutenant's Woman* sees ordinary people as relatively uncomplicated, and only a privileged few, such as Charles and Sarah, as trapped in existentialist agonies over their personal destiny. Thus the novel might be said to echo the dualism of the many and the few that Fowles outlined in *The Aristos* and presented allegorically in *The Collector* (see Chapter 6). This reading is reinforced by the gulf between the educational levels of the two couples, which permits them different degrees of cultural reference. Intertextual allusions of the sort made by Charles at Carslake's Barn are not permitted to Sam and Mary. The narrator points out that Mary has never heard of Catullus (400), nor has Sam heard of Faust (405).

Charles, by contrast, is acutely aware of how his social status leads to uncomfortable personal dilemmas, when he contemplates life as part of the Freeman empire upon his intended marriage to Ernestina. According to the narrator, Charles rejects

Mr Freeman's job offer partly out of laziness, cowardice and snobbery,

> But there was one noble element in his rejection: a sense that the pursuit of money was an insufficient purpose in life. [. . .] a sense that choosing to be nothing – to have nothing but prickles – was the last saving grace of a gentleman; his last freedom, almost. It came to him very clearly: If I ever set foot in that place I am done for. (284–5)

Charles's social class makes his relationship to Freeman's one of agonized choice, whereas for Sam it is one of economic necessity, sharpened by his lingering sense that he could achieve more if he were given the capital to work independently. Charles is rendered hypersensitive by the existential threat that he perceives from Mr Freeman's store in Oxford Street: the colours of the clothes within the window 'seemed almost to stain the air around them, so intense, so *nouveau riche* were they' (284). He is aware, also, that his class is doomed by the social Darwinism of the survival of the fittest. He feels that the trappings of his rank are like the obsolete armour of a dinosaur: worse, he is a 'living fossil' (281). What Charles does *not* do, unlike Sam, is to calculate his relationship to Freeman's in exact financial terms. He has no need to. There is, then, an enormous irony of social class in Sam's creation of the slogan 'Freeman's for Choice', for he, the worker, has none: only the gentleman Charles has the financial, as well as existentialist, choice available to him to walk away from commerce.

Although their degrees of freedom are different, Sam, in choosing to accept Freeman's job offer, and Charles, in rejecting the very same thing, are following Marx's definition of history, in that they are acting '*in pursuit of their ends*' (*FLW*, 445: emphasis in original). Thus biographical life stands in a microcosmic relationship to social history, as its qualities reflect society's broader trends and ideological undercurrents. In conversation with Charles, Mr Freeman rejects entirely the idea that mankind is descended from apes, but says he has reflected on the Darwinian idea of adaptation in order for a species to survive, and finds merit in it (277). His meaning is both general and specific: first, that any business must adapt to changing trade conditions to survive; second, that for Charles, a position in the business would be a necessary adaptation to his marrying into the Freeman family without an estate and title (as these have been effectively taken away from him by his uncle's marriage). It is this discussion that sparks off Charles's later pessimistic thoughts about the doomed status of the gentleman class.

Darwinism has a clear link with Marxism in that both theories claim that the world is based on struggle, meaning the competition either between species or between social classes for the same resources: indeed, Marx wanted to dedicate volume I of *Capital* to Darwin (Acheson, 1998, 33). *The French Lieutenant's Woman* offers a dialectical opposition between classes in which the leisured aristocracy is doomed to lose to the hard-working bourgeoisie and emerging lower-middle class. For Charles, the only resolution to this dialectic is to abandon it altogether, and to seek existential freedom by making his own choices in a manner determined not by class or convention but by authentic self-knowledge. To some extent, he achieves this in the open ending of Chapter 61. Sam, by contrast, is caught in another, more prosaic dialectic, a struggle between the roles of servant and employee, in which the latter is bound to win: as one social species dies, the other grows.

A Marxist reading of the novel might find its celebration of individual, existential growth inimical to positive social change. It seems that the novel interprets the epigraph from *Zur Judenfrage* about the restoration of human relationships 'to man himself' first in personal terms and only second as a social statement. Politically, Fowles was always on the left, but had been criticized as a reactionary, even worse a 'crypto-fascist' (*A*, 8). The differences between the fates of Sam and Mary, Sarah and Charles, and the options open to all four, may make *The French Lieutenant's Woman* seem like an elitist book, which regards only those with inner gifts (the Few, or the *aristoi*, in Fowles's terms) as able to achieve existential development. Simon Loveday, for instance, argues that 'it is hard not to see a scarcely veiled snobbery at work' in the differing treatments of Charles and

Sam: 'one longs for the day when Fowles will choose his *aristoi* from somewhere other than the aristocracy' (Loveday, 1985, 67). Fowles's later novel *A Maggot* goes some way towards answering Loveday, as its main *aristos* is the poor prostitute Rebecca Hocknell (see Chapter 6): moreover, Sarah Woodruff should surely have given Loveday pause, as she is far from aristocratic, and may also have become a prostitute when alone in London. She joins the artistically and intellectually privileged Rossetti household at the end, but only as a form of servant, or salaried muse. Although in *The French Lieutenant's Woman* only Sarah and Charles achieve existential liberation, and the vast majority of the characters are incapable of it, or unwilling to seek it (like the educated, sophisticated but ultimately conservative and comfortable Grogan), Sarah's relatively low status, and Charles's fall from his high position into disgrace, show that the novel sees the *aristoi* as those with existential rather than social privilege. Perhaps the best defence of the novel here comes from Fowles himself, with his point, made in *The Aristos*, that the dividing line between the Few and the Many runs *within* individuals (see Chapter 6). Thus Charles and Sarah have the potential for dull conformity – as shown by Charles's marriage to Ernestina in the false ending of Chapter 44, and their replication of a conventional Victorian family in the closed ending of Chapter 60 – and Sam has the potential for free thought and action, which leads him, albeit impotently, to question Charles and Mr Freeman and their right to determine his destiny.

EPIGRAPHS AND THE VICTORIAN SAGE

Chapter 28 begins with two epigraphs. The first is from Arthur Hugh Clough's 'Poem' of 1840, and includes the lines, 'Assumptions, hasty, crude, and vain, / Full oft to use will Science deign'. The second comes from Matthew Arnold's 'The Lake' of 1853: 'Again I spring to make my choice; / Again in tones of ire / I hear a God's tremendous voice – "Be counsell'd, and retire!" ' (223). Epigraphs such as this do not stand outside the action of the novel; they form part of an integrated system of commentaries on the plot, and give prompts to the reader, just as they might in a Victorian novel. The Clough epigraph, for instance, is clearly intended as a negative comment on Grogan and Matthaei's assumptions, made in the same chapter, about hysterical women: it suggests not only that the doctors are in error, but also that the reader's opinion of Sarah may be wrong. However, if because of the epigraph the reader disagrees with Grogan's patriarchal views on Sarah, it is because he or she has been *told* to do so, and is responding to a quoted fragment of the very Victorian didacticism that Charles, in his agonized concern and love for Sarah, is trying to repudiate. The Arnold epigraph is similar. The poem advises against hasty judgement. As with the Clough fragment, if the reader accepts the point made, then they may resist Grogan's reading of Sarah as a hysteric, but they are also accepting the authority of Arnold and finally of 'God's tremendous voice', the discourse of the ultimate patriarch. Thus *The French Lieutenant's Woman* uses Victorian epigraphs conventionally, and yet allows the reader to question their function, as they are in many ways complicit in the repressive discourses of religion, medicine, and so on, which the text seeks to question.

The many major Victorian authors mentioned in the main body of the novel, as well as in footnotes and in epigraphs, are cited not only for their work, but also for their names: they are enlisted as powerful signs of the Victorian and the Literary (or the Scientific). They may be called Victorian sages, in the sense given by John Holloway:

> all of them sought (among other things) to express notions about the world, man's situation in it, and how he should live. Their work reflects an outlook on life, an outlook which for most or perhaps all of them was partly philosophical and partly moral. (Holloway, 1953, 1)

The sages' moral interest and world-view often leads to a didactic tone in their work. This may, to some readers, make *The French Lieutenant's Woman* itself seem didactic. However, the novel alludes to such sages not in order to reinforce an overarching message, but to perform its own parodic series of variations upon nineteenth-century pedagogy and wisdom in order to 'reconstruct, represent, and "colonize" the cultural milieu of the Victorian age' for its own ends (Salami, 1992, 107):

> The novel's telescoping of two centuries may be understood as Fowles's effort to textualize, appropriate, and rewrite the nineteenth century itself. Under the auspices of that historical destabilization which the book effects, allusions to Victorian thinkers and scientists like Mayhew, Mill, Darwin, and Marx abound. The narrator as authorial surrogate chooses, edits, and situates these quotations for his own purposes, and in so doing he constructs his own version of nineteenth-century social and intellectual history. (Cooper, 1991, 135)

As Cooper suggests, the novel's appropriations of the Victorian canon are not always consistent, and the actual ideas and arguments of great nineteenth-century writers are often deliberately distorted or obscured. For instance, three stanzas of Arnold's 'A Farewell' are quoted as the epigraph to Chapter 22 (183). The epigraph reproduces only the stanzas dealing with 'will like a dividing spear' and the relative rarity of 'love' (Arnold, 1950, 178). The later sections claiming that the lovers will eventually unite 'in the eternal Father's smile' are omitted: God, or 'He, who sees us through and through' is suppressed (179). The contradiction created by this humanist censorship of a Christian text is artfully buried, and cannot be discovered unless the reader turns to Arnold's poem itself. The novel's treatment of Arnold's 'To Marguerite' is similar. The lyric is quoted extensively in Chapter 58 (407–12). The narrator describes it as 'perhaps the noblest short poem of the whole Victorian era' (408). In a footnote, he gives its title as 'To Marguerite' (1853)' (409). The date is used to fix the poem in the period of the novel, and implies that it is traceable to one point in time. There is no suggestion that '1853' indicates one version of the lyric rather than another. However, there were several versions; the narrator cites the poem in an early edition, before another section was added in 1857 (Arnold, 1950, 180). This new section of the poem claims that the men who loved Marguerite were 'happier' than she, because they 'were through faith released / From isolation without end / Prolong'd;

nor knew, although not less / Alone than thou, their loneliness' (181). There is an obvious reason for the narrator's omission of these lines; they claim that the comfort of religion can compensate for the loneliness of solitude, whereas in *The French Lieutenant's Woman* the emphasis of the final ending is on Charles's growth towards self-knowledge via the understanding of his own lonely existential freedom. So when the narrator chooses the parts of his sources he wishes to show the reader, he selects those which conform to his own priorities.

Arnold is made to signify according to the needs of the text at any given moment. At the end of the novel, 'To Marguerite' and the narrator's gloss on the epigraph from the *Notebooks* (445) are used to construct Arnold as a form of early existentialist, whose credo is 'True piety is *acting what one knows*' (440: emphasis in original). Elsewhere, though, the novel makes him seem conservative, and representative of mainstream opinion of his time. One such instance is the citation of *Culture and Anarchy* in the epigraph to Chapter 51:

> More and more [. . .] men, all over the country, are beginning to assert and put in practice an Englishman's right to do what he likes [. . .] threaten as he likes, smash as he likes. All this, I say, tends to anarchy. (Arnold, 1948, 76; cited in *FLW*, 370)

Through these contradictory quotations, Fowles's novel enacts the twentieth century's dual construction of Arnold. First, in 'To Marguerite', he appears as a typical post-Romantic lyricist whose project is 'a quest for the lost wholeness and transcendence of the imaginary' (Belsey, 1980, 123); and second, in *Culture and Anarchy*, he is a reactionary cultural theorist concerned merely with the need for 'the cultivation of individuals, or the development of a class of finely tuned sensibilities, or the renaissance of interest in the classics' (Said, 1991, 10). Arnold is given great significance (his words are allowed to end the novel), and yet he is also marginalized by being largely relegated to footnotes and epigraphs. He becomes a secondary element of the text, a peripheral vehicle which enables it to pursue its own concerns.

The French Lieutenant's Woman's citations of its Victorian sources are re-enactments rather than references: they form part of an extended, and often self-contradictory, pattern of performances by the narrator. Take, for instance, the novel's allusions to Charles Darwin and *The Origin of Species*. In Chapter 8, the narrator tells us that Charles Smithson 'called himself a Darwinist, and yet he had not really understood Darwin' (*FLW*, 53). He holds an ammonite fossil in his hand, and yet does not realize that a species can become extinct, as opposed to an individual. Charles 'can hardly be blamed' for his thoughts (54). He is not making an accidental, idiosyncratic error here, but is allegedly reading Darwin in a typically Victorian fashion. Darwin, too, is depicted as restricted by the conceptual horizons of his age. Charles had not understood Darwin, but 'nor had Darwin himself' (53). It seems that the novel is casting Darwin as philosophically and sociologically blind: just as Charles is prepared to forget those parts of *The Origin of Species* that are inconvenient to him, insofar as they do not suit his theory of himself as one of those 'naturally selected' as superior (159), the novel implies that Darwin too forgot or never understood the full social and philosophical implications of his theories, because he was still too closely bound to the philosophies that informed preceding natural-historical models: 'Even Darwin never quite shook off the Swedish fetters' of Linnaean theory (54).

This picture of Darwin is not permitted to remain stable, because it is contradicted elsewhere. Later in the novel we read that Charles is able not only to conceive of the extinction of species, but also, and more importantly, to apply Darwinian theory to the social formation around him: 'he felt that the enormous apparatus rank required a gentleman to erect around himself was like the massive armour that had been the death warrant of so many ancient saurian species' (281). At another stage, the narrator openly states that Victorian thinkers were able to apply Darwin's ideas to human society:

Darwinism, as its shrewder opponents realized, let open the floodgates to something far more serious than the undermining

of the Biblical account of the origins of man; its deepest implications lay in the direction of determinism and behaviourism,
that is, towards philosophies that reduce morality to a
hypocrisy and duty to a straw hut in a hurricane. (119)

These two citations show that the novel's treatment of Darwin
has changed since Chapter 8. Not only did Darwin's ideas have
sociological relevance, but their 'deepest implications' were also
comprehensible both to his educated supporters, such as Charles,
and to his 'shrewder opponents'. It would seem unlikely that,
given such relatively widespread comprehension of his theories,
Darwin himself could have remained ignorant of their social
implications. Nevertheless, *The French Lieutenant's Woman* does
not enlighten us on this matter. It is left to the reader to decide
how to make Darwin signify, and how to interpret the text's
re-enactment of *The Origin of Species*.

The novel also incorporates Darwinian ideas into its structure.
Not only is the narrator evolving and adapting Darwin by
making him signify in different ways, but he is also evolving his
own work (and, by implication, evolving himself). The narrator
portrays his text as a naturally selected member of its own
species. The epigraph to Chapter 50 is taken from *The Origin of
Species*. One can, in the context of *The French Lieutenant's
Woman*, read the word 'forms' as signifying textual structures as
well as biological species:

I think it inevitably follows, that as new species in the course
of time are formed through natural selection, others will
become rarer and rarer, and finally extinct. The forms which
stand in closest competition with those undergoing mod-
ification and improvement will naturally suffer most.
(Darwin, 1985, 154; cited in *FLW*, 360)

The French Lieutenant's Woman is a neo-Darwinian text that
urges its own evolutionary credentials upon the reader by drawing
attention to such mutations as the dual ending (see Rankin, 1973,
cited in Chapter 4). The narrator attempts to ensure that the
reader will see this as something radically new, representing an

evolution of the novel form, through his emphasis on his own refusal to indulge in 'fight-fixing' (390). He declares that he is choosing the order of the two endings at random, by tossing a coin. This process is analogous to the 'random mutations in the nucleic acid helix caused by natural radiation' mentioned in the first epigraph to the final chapter (440). The narrator refers to the discourse of evolution in order to present his novel as the fittest type, a survivor, but ironizes this performance through the flippancy of his use and misuse of *The Origin of Species* and associated texts. The narrator-cum-impresario who tosses the coin is 'a very minor figure – as minimal, in fact, as a gamma-ray particle' (440). Although he is the tiny dose of radiation that modifies the helix of the novel's DNA at random, and thus supposedly permits it to evolve, he is also the actor-mythologist who leaves interpretation open to the reader, and sometimes hides as much as he reveals, reading his sources in mutually contradictory ways. Like a Brechtian actor, the narrator is able 'to appear strange and even surprising to the audience [. . .] by looking strangely at himself and his work' (Brecht, 1974, 92). *The French Lieutenant's Woman* defamiliarizes the Victorian canon: the reader is forced to look again at Arnold, Darwin, Marx and other significant nineteenth-century figures, and to realize how they can never be accessed directly but are always filtered through editing and interpretation and are mediated by the huge historical gap between the nineteenth century and today. This is one of the novel's most powerful alienation effects.

TIME, SPACE, IDENTITY

Sam and Mary are lovers whose difference is not of status or wealth (as with Charles and Sarah, and Charles and Ernestina) but of region. Their social roles are similar, but the geographical divide between them is vast:

> Their coming together was fraught with almost as many obstacles as if he had been an Eskimo and she, a Zulu. They had barely a common language, so often did they not understand what the other had just said. (129)

Although Sam's London sophistication clashes with Mary's relative rural innocence, each is attracted to what is distinctive about the other. Such differences of region, nation and ethnicity help to shape *The French Lieutenant's Woman* and its inhabitants. Despite the close focus of the text on Lyme (and later London), the characters come from, and travel to, a surprisingly wide number of places and countries. Grogan is Irish, Varguennes French, Sam from London and Mary from Dorset; Charles visits mainland Europe for travel and sexual adventure, and then finds exile in America after Sarah, who is now dwelling in London, seemingly abandons him. The narrator's references to Matthaei, Freud and Marx add a German element to the novel's intertextual range, and Fowles's long-standing interest in French culture lies behind its allusions to medieval romance (see Chapter 1).

One of the novel's main intertexts has a plot driven by ethnic difference, which Fowles translates into existential alienation. The story of the melancholy Sarah was, according to Fowles, partly based on *Ourika* by Claire de Duras, a French novel of 1824, in which Ourika, a black girl, is adopted by a white family and tries to fit into pre-Revolutionary French society, but eventually realizes she cannot do so, as her ethnicity makes her unmarriageable except to a venal exploiter. Fowles claimed that *Ourika* was 'the germ of *The French Lieutenant's Woman*' (*W*, 59): the protagonist's 'African figure [. . .] was very active in my unconscious' during the composition of the novel (*W*, 60). By coincidence, or subconscious appropriation by Fowles, the male protagonist in each case has the same name, Charles. Doris Y. Kadish has examined Fowles's debt to Duras from a feminist perspective, claiming that he often diminishes *Ourika*'s 'treatment of feminine voice, vision, identity, sexuality, and community' (Kadish, 1997, 75). However, against this, it is possible to argue that Fowles reworks Ourika's sense of alienation caused by gender and ethnic stereotyping in a relatively subtle way that reflects Sarah's attempt to realize her own identity. Sarah, of course, is white, but her association with Varguennes, and therefore with the stereotype of the French as licentious, makes it easier for the parochial citizens of Lyme to turn her into a pariah: unlike Ourika, though, Sarah *wants* to be ostracized. Her choice of a black, masculine garment 'like a man's riding-coat' (15) suggests a deliberate flouting of fashion and gender codes right from the start of the novel. Her constant staring out to sea is also highly antisocial behaviour, suggesting a profound desire to escape Englishness and the restrictions that go with it: to Sarah, the watery void with its promise of foreign shores is more interesting than the prosaic view of Lyme behind her, which stands for the provincial Victorian world she is part of, but wants to transcend. Much the same might be said of her walks to the Undercliff, a place where solitude and an unmediated relationship with nature are both possible, in contrast to the suffocating regime of Mrs Poulteney's house.

As she separates herself from Lyme, and attaches herself to Charles, Sarah is moving between different spaces, which hold for her the promise of different temporal rhythms and varying degrees of freedom. As novelistic devices, these spaces are examples of what Mikhail Bakhtin has called the 'chronotope', or time–space arrangement. The Undercliff, with its Arcadian associations of untrammelled nature (although seen through the lens of evolutionary theory, as we saw in the scene with the wren singing to Charles), represents a development of the 'bucolic-pastoral-idyllic' chronotope, in which time

> possesses its own definite semicyclical rhythm, but it has fused bodily with a specific insular idyllic landscape, one worked out in meticulous detail. This is a dense and fragrant time, like honey, a time of intimate lovers' scenes and lyric outpourings, a time saturated with its own strictly limited, sealed-off segment of nature's space. (Bakhtin, 1981, 103)

The repeated trysts between Charles and Sarah represent the lovers' meetings referred to by Bakhtin, and we have already seen modified forms of lyrical outpouring in the Undercliff, when Charles finds himself quoting Sappho to represent his feelings, and when he hears the wren's song and the narrator compares him to Pisanello's St Eustace. Because this is a post-Freudian, existentialist novel rather than an ancient Greek poem of the sort

Bakhtin is writing about, the 'insular idyllic landscape' of the Undercliff is insular in the psychological sense as well as the geographical one of being isolated (from the Latin *insula*, or 'island'). It is a chronotope where pastoralism meets introspection and personal insight. Even in the 1960s, says the narrator, people get lost there, and cannot believe, once they see it on a map, that 'their sense of isolation – and if the weather be bad, desolation – could have seemed so great' (70). That is to say, the Undercliff is a place where rational considerations of measurement and analysis (based on an objective sense of space–time) cannot apply: on his first visit there, Charles finds himself 'forced [. . .] into anti-science' (71). Once there, the human subject is caught, for better or worse, in a 'strictly limited, sealed-off segment of nature's space'. The Undercliff is also an instance of one of Fowles's favourite chronotopes, the *domaine* or *bonne vaux*, taken from French medieval romance, and typically an isolated, enchanted clearing in a forest where the protagonist learns much about his or her identity and personal quest (Conchis's villa in *The Magus* is at the centre of one such *domaine*: see Chapter 6). The *domaines* of Fowles's fiction are 'privileged and almost sacred places where [. . .] the imagination can roam freely' (Loveday, 1985, 4).

The transitions the characters make between chronotopes are just as significant as the chronotopes themselves. Journeys of all kinds in *The French Lieutenant's Woman* can be read as metaphors for intellectual or existential travel and choices made to live differently. Fowles has taken 'ideas are the only motherland', his own translation of a sentence from *Ourika*, as 'the most succinct summary I know of what I believe' (*W*, 27). When Grogan discovers that Charles is a fellow Darwinian, he grips his hand 'as if he were Crusoe, and Charles, Man Friday' (158). Thus the shipwrecked sailor of Defoe's novel *Robinson Crusoe* (first published 1719) and his native companion, two dwellers in isolation, are used to suggest the sense of separateness felt by Grogan and Charles, who consider themselves intellectual émigrés from Victorian convention. References to spatial distance, ethnic difference and travel are part of the novel's attempts to address political and intellectual dialogues, between, say, Darwinism and the dominant Victorian ideology.

Reading the novel with special attention to such details as time, space and nation leads to insights about its underlying ideas. For instance, Charles finds himself sexually frustrated, but only because he cannot bring himself *to go abroad* to seek a prostitute: until his encounter in London with the unfortunately named Sarah, he finds himself unable to visit prostitutes in England, after a traumatic early experience. This, to say the least, looks odd. Why is England so important to Charles's sexual morality? What is it about either his perception of his own country or his sense of himself as an Englishman that makes paying for sex acceptable in France or Spain but not at home? In *The French Lieutenant's Woman*, space and nation have a symbolic dimension, so that they stand for hegemonic and marginal ideas, and discourses in competition. Charles cannot visit a prostitute and remain within the safe environment of the part-ironic, part-conventional Victorian ideology he still wants to inhabit. To him, England and Englishness are symbols of this ideology: thus to pay an *English* woman to sleep with him is to expose the venal infrastructure and hypocritical evasions that allow that ideology to sustain itself. Escape from this dominant discourse is possible, but only under strict conditions that prevent it from being threatened, i.e. when Charles is in the role of a traveller, and when the women are not English, and return to England and chastity is guaranteed.

The connection between place and ideology is made clearer when Charles, with a degree of vanity and hypocrisy, connects his frequent travels with a sense of felt difference from others:

> It was a fixed article of Charles's creed that he was not like the great majority of his peers and contemporaries. That was why he had travelled so much; he found English society too hidebound, English solemnity too solemn, English thought too moralistic, English religion too bigoted. (128)

Tellingly, it as it this early point in the narrative that Charles first realizes he is attracted to Sarah. Even later in the novel, when the trap of English moralism seems to have been avoided because Charles has rejected the 'too conventional' Ernestina (128), and

Sarah Woodruff has replaced Victorian convention as a focus for his ideals, he still cannot satisfy his sexual needs with English prostitutes – his visit to the London Sarah ends in a fit of vomiting when he finds out her name and thus feels acute guilt. The pattern is only really broken when Charles, having been taught something of his true worth by Sarah Woodruff, and having learned about the 'unfair because remediable bias in society' (392) that forces many women into prostitution, visits America. Using prostitutes there does not occur to him and is never mentioned, and instead he sees the new country as a focal point of women's liberation.

Charles's two sexual encounters with the two Sarahs (only one of which ends in intercourse) take place in an enclosed, urban chronotope: that of the hotel room or lodging-house, whose temporal associations are with transience, instability and motion, and whose space is cramped and characterized by proximity to others who dwell uncomfortably close and who are sometimes bent on surveillance and/or moral censure. When Charles reaches the prostitute's lodgings, the cab driver has already shown his disapproval by looking straight ahead and down the street, as if the sight of a man so degraded as to be a prostitute's client is unbearable: 'Charles was glad not to be looked at; and yet felt quite as unspeakable as this ancient cab-driver seemed determined to make him feel' (299). Once in the house, the close proximity of 'obscure voices' (299), the errand-boy Harry, who had 'evidently been trained not to stare' (302), and the prostitute's baby daughter Mary serve to sharpen his guilt. Similarly, in the ironically named Endicott's Family Hotel, Mrs Endicott acts as a gatekeeper who judges visitors and clients by their financial, rather than moral, worth: like the London prostitute shouting coarsely for Harry, she calls 'with a surprising violence' for her errand-runner Betty Anne, who takes him up three flights of steep stairs and a 'mournful corridor' (332). Even when he is undressing so rapidly that a button falls off, he remembers to go and lock the door (337): after having sex with Sarah, he imagines Ernestina looking on 'mournfully', and Mr Freeman hitting him across the face (338). His sense that he is 'the last man alive, infinitely isolated' (338) is undermined by his feeling of being watched. This sensation is heightened by the confined, semi-public chronotope of the room, in which space is rented and time paid for, as with the lodgings of the prostitute. This is, then, the chronotopic opposite of the pastoral, fertile, isolated Undercliff. In the novel, identity is contingent upon time and place: despite his quest for existential freedom, who Charles is depends on where and when he is. Although the dependency of selfhood upon location may seem deterministic, in fact it can also promise freedom, as a contingent identity can be a rapidly changing one: Charles's trysts with Sarah in the Undercliff, standing in contrast to his stilted meetings with Ernestina in Lyme, bear witness to this.

In the last analysis, *The French Lieutenant's Woman* will respond to a reading based on one thesis (for example, a Marxist or feminist approach): but any such interpretation will have to sideline much of the novel's content and ignore a good deal of its complexity. It is a text that cannot be neatly pigeonholed. Although many critics have produced informative, and sometimes compelling, readings, Fowles's novel has enough depth to continue to demand analysis. The following chapter will trace the novel's reception, showing some of the main trends in the evolving critical debate.

TOPICS FOR FURTHER DISCUSSION

Dates

As part of its examination of the unstable relationship between time, place and identity, the novel often treats calendar time sceptically and ironically. Sometimes, precise dates are given: Ernestina reads poetry to Charles on the evening of 6 April 1867, a week after a House of Commons motion to give women equal voting rights (the motion failed). On other occasions, the given dates contradict themselves. Ernestina dies on the day Hitler invaded Poland in 1939 (33), and yet Charles 'finally survived her by a decade (and earnestly mourned her throughout it)' (325). This means that Charles dies at the unlikely age of 114. There is clear scope for linking such a playful treatment of historical time to the novel's play with its Victorian sources: to what extent is the novel refusing to take them seriously? Does the narrator's occasional precision over dates help to locate the action convincingly in the Victorian era, or does it seem arbitrary and artificial? Do the links made between Victorian events and the novel's plots suggest connections between them? For example, does Ernestina's refusal to take the idea of the Commons motion on women's voting rights (115) seriously help to suggest how typical she is of her era?

Writing

Ernestina keeps a diary, Charles has published several essays in fashionable magazines, and a scientific monograph, but refuses the opportunity to publish a travel book as there seemed 'something decidedly too much like hard work and sustained concentration' in authorship (21). Later on, separated from Sarah, he writes poetry: although 'he would rather have died than show it to anyone else' (408), the narrator offers eight lines of it to the reader, then another whole poem, of which one line is 'really not too bad' (417). Why does the narrator make Charles such a scientific and literary dilettante? This question could be answered with reference to his evolutionary position as part of a dying breed: the gentleman. Charles's writing might also be linked to the text's pervasive commentary on literariness. For instance, how do Charles's efforts at composition, and what we know of their motivation, compare with the narrator's comments about novel-writing in Chapter 13? Tellingly, Sarah Woodruff also writes, but only in terse notes to Charles, one of three words (Endicott's Family Hotel), and the other in French to defeat casual readers, giving her location at Carslake's Barn. What does Sarah's taciturnity suggest, when compared to Charles's literariness? What does each character's writing signify about them?

Drugs and addiction

The novel contains a number of references to drugs, including alcohol, opium and tobacco. In America, upon first hearing that Sarah has been found, Charles 'lit himself a stogy', a type of cigar (418). Drugs are used at other crisis points: abandoned by

Sam, Charles 'spent his rage on the empty brandy-glass' (373). Ernestina, having had her engagement broken off by Charles, is put to sleep by Grogan, probably with opium (374). Charles goes to Grogan after receiving Sarah's note, having fortified himself with a gill – six modern measures – of cobbler, or brandy and sherry combined, that he drinks in less than five minutes (203). He then reads Matthaei under the influence of the cobbler and Grogan's brandy. After his encounter with Mr Freeman in London, where the manufacturer tries to get him to join the family business, Charles sees 'Hope? Courage? Determination? I am afraid not. He saw a bowl of milk punch and a pint of champagne' (287). There follows a drunken evening at his club, which culminates in the visit to the prostitute Sarah, where a bottle of cheap Hock makes him vomit after she declares her name (304). Alcohol is associated with failure or indecision for Charles, and sobriety with insight. Disgusted by the prostitutes' dance at the brothel, he finds that 'as the clothes fell, so did his drunkenness' (296). Charles, after meeting Grogan, decides (against the doctor's advice) to visit Sarah, but only after the brandy and cobbler have worn off, 'leaving Charles only with a profound sense of guilt' at his own behaviour, that soon translates itself into an understanding of Sarah's true sanity, once he has re-read Matthaei when sober (230), and rejected Grogan's claim that Sarah is '*addicted to melancholia as one becomes addicted to opium*' (153: emphasis in original). The same drug is used regularly by Mrs Poulteney, who has become an addict, because laudanum was 'a very near equivalent of our own age's sedative pills' (94).

Are drugs, and the discourse of dependency, symbols of the Victorian conventionality that would hold Charles back? Whether in drunken excess in London, or in alcohol-fuelled masculine camaraderie with Grogan, Charles uses drugs at moments when his existential progress has halted. Why? After being rejected as a husband by Sarah, even though they have slept together, Charles seeks a narcotic banishment of his painful self-awareness: 'His greatest desire was darkness, invisibility, *oblivion*, in which to regain calm' (344: emphasis added). What does this desire signify? The theme of drugs might productively be linked to the novel's treatment of gender, especially to the relative sobriety enforced on the women (the novel's one female addict, Mrs Poulteney, thinks of her drug as medicinal). Even the prostitute Sarah encourages Charles to drink all the wine he has paid for, rather than sharing it with him. Why are the women in the novel so much less inclined to recreational drug use than the men? Do other forms of obsessive behaviour replace drug addiction for some of the female characters?

DISCUSSION QUESTIONS

1. The writer and critic A. S. Byatt has claimed that in her own celebrated historical novel, *Possession* (winner of the Booker Prize in 1990), she wanted to rescue 'the complicated Victorian thinkers from modern diminishing parodies like those of Fowles' (Byatt, 2001, 79). Is Byatt right to believe that Fowles is reductive in his approach to Victorian intellectuals like Arnold, Darwin and Marx, and the Victorian age in general? How does *Possession* compare to *The French Lieutenant's Woman* in its highly self-conscious re-creation of a Victorian world? Which do you find more effective?
2. Charles and Sarah are continually compared to modern characters – for example, in the references to Sarah's having a computer in her heart or to Charles as a computer scientist (*FLW*, 57, 285). To what extent are Charles and Sarah modern, rather than Victorian, in the way they think and act?
3. Charles and Sarah fight against the society around them, whereas many of the minor characters – for example, Mrs Poulteney, Mr Freeman and Dr Grogan – seem in different ways to personify the conservative values that hold the protagonists back. Are the two existentialist heroes totally distinct from the other people around them, or do characters such as Sam, Mary and Ernestina have existentialist ambitions, even if they are not fully aware of them?
4. The novel makes a vast number of references to literature and culture – for example, in the epigraphs and the narrator's footnotes. Do these detract from the main narrative, or add to it? Would the novel have been better without them? Did Fowles risk accusations of elitism and pretension by including so many references, or do they strengthen the novel? If so, how?

5. Charles, travelling to America in the wake of the Civil War of 1861–5, senses 'the strange vastness and frustrated energy of this split nation' (*FLW*, 415). He also sees how far advanced the women's movement is there. What does the novel tell us about the USA, and what does Charles find there? How do nineteenth-century America and England compare in the novel? Is it significant that Charles believes that Sarah Woodruff would have felt herself at home in the USA?

CHAPTER 4

CRITICAL RECEPTION

Every significant novel has a long and complex life story that begins with conception, preliminary notes, composition, the final draft, and then the author's consultations with agents and editors. After publication, reviews appear, then conference papers, journal articles and eventually academic monographs as the text's critical reputation grows. In the mature phase of the novel's life, there are successive editions, film or television adaptations, and entry into the school or university curriculum. Finally, long after the author's death, the most highly regarded text might find itself enjoyed by future generations as part of the literature of the past. The story of *The French Lieutenant's Woman* is far from over, and it is impossible to guess where the novel will end up, and for how many generations it will be read. Nevertheless, if a classic text possesses not only 'intrinsic qualities that endure' but also 'an openness to accommodation which keeps [it] alive under endlessly varying dispositions' (Kermode, 1975, 44), then *The French Lieutenant's Woman* is close to being a classic already, as its widely varying critical interpretations over nearly 40 years show.

REVIEWS AND EARLY READINGS

When writing *The French Lieutenant's Woman*, Fowles had no idea how it would be received, but feared 'vitriolic reviews' (*W*, 25). In fact, the novel's British notices were more lukewarm than vitriolic, although they mostly recognized the strength of

Fowles's performance: Fowles thought them 'all bouquet-and-reservation; damning with faint praise' (*J II*, 60). A typical example came from the *Guardian*, whose reviewer believed 'Symbols and allegory stain almost every page of this long, puzzling book', and found Fowles's references to sociology 'now and again pretentious' and yet recommended the novel as 'rewarding' if 'Consumed slowly' (Trevor, 1969). The *Daily Telegraph*'s critic believed Fowles's readers would find themselves 'vastly beguiled and/or irritated by turn' and yet would, in the end, applaud such a 'tour-de-force' (Berridge, 1969). The *Observer* found the central characters 'rather manipulated and over-representative', and believed Fowles's self-referential passages diminished both author and characters; however, the reviewer did concede that the book was 'a remarkable performance as well as an interesting exercise' (Wall, 1969). In *The Times*, Mary Conroy complained, 'It's fun, but it doesn't add up to a novel', because Fowles had underestimated the sophistication of Victorian fictional conventions and thus oversimplified his subject matter (Conroy, 1969). Fowles found such reviews 'full of misunderstandings, the voice of the literary establishment' (*J II*, 60). A few, however, recognized the significance of the book. In *The Times Literary Supplement*, D. A. N. Jones concluded that Fowles had 'found a way, in this tour de force, to emulate the great Victorians, to supplement them without patronage' (Jones, 1969). James Price in *The New Statesman* declared that Fowles had created a 'crammed and complex novel' with Victorian fiction merely 'a lovingly handled framework' for his 'larger purpose'. The result was 'a splendid, lucid, profoundly satisfying work of art' (Price, 1969).

The French Lieutenant's Woman appeared in the USA a few months later, in November 1969. The reviews were far better than in Britain. Writing in *The New York Times*, Ian Watt hailed the novel as a great improvement on Fowles's earlier novels, because it combined sensitivity with philosophical insight, thus managing to be 'both richly English and convincingly existential' as well as 'immensely interesting, attractive and human' (Watt, 1969, 1). And yet, at the same time, Fowles broke with the conventional limits set on the role of the narrator, to challenge received ideas of 'the authority of the novelist in the new intellectual ecology' (74). Watt's final impression was 'of pleasure and even, on occasion, awe' (74). In the same newspaper, Christopher Lehmann-Haupt astutely anticipated how the technical experimentation of the novel would engage a popular audience, as not only did the opening promise a strong plot, but it also implied 'something will happen to the form of the book as well. And the prospect adds immeasurably to the suspense' (Lehmann-Haupt, 1969, 45). *Contemporary Literature* recognized how *The French Lieutenant's Woman* was indebted to the past and yet could stake out new ground: it was 'a parody of a partly superseded literary mode' but revealed 'the illumination possible when the creative imagination has wrought a new form to embody its riches' (McDowell, 1970, 431). The *National Review* viewed the novel's experiments as an extension of tradition rather than a departure from it: although Fowles seemed not to do what was expected of a novelist, 'his sleight-of-hand is really the novel's ancient business of beguiling us' (Davenport, 1969, 1223). The *New Republic* found the book nearly perfect, but not quite: 'A flawless book? No, Fowles is compulsively didactic.' However, he had achieved 'a miracle of sorts' (Chase, 1969, 24). In his diary, Fowles played down the Americans' admiration, finding 'something faintly hysterical' about it, as if the reviewers were 'slightly dazzled' by the book's language (*J II*, 66). It was perhaps not a coincidence that one of the least positive reviews published in the USA came from a leading British critic, Christopher Ricks, in *The New York Review of Books*. Ricks saw the novel's combination of modern and Victorian conventions as 'taunting and incisive' but believed that its parodies of Victorian writing sometimes amounted to cliché: 'Vacant phrasing sinks under heavy irony' (Ricks, 1970, n. p.).

However, such reservations were to be overwhelmed by American popular taste. *Time* magazine accurately predicted that *The French Lieutenant's Woman*'s originality would make it a bestseller: the reviewer boldly stated that it was 'more truly inventive and contemporary than a whole shelf of campus comings-of-age or suburban wife-swapping sagas' (1969). As a result of such positive notices and of Fowles's three-week promotional tour, the novel sold extremely well in the USA. Some

100,000 copies were printed there in the first week after publication (*J II*, 69) and it reached number one in *The New York Times* bestseller list in February 1970, and remained on the list a year after publication (*J II*, 77, 99). In Britain, by contrast, Fowles noted that sales had been disappointing: the novel had hardly been noticed since the reviews, and had sunk 'like a stone in a rough sea' (*J II*, 63). However, the world would eventually catch up with America, especially after the release of the film version in 1981 (see Chapter 5): by 1984, total sales *excluding* the USA were over one million (Loveday, 1985, xii).

Academic researchers were, as always, slower than reviewers to come to their conclusions. Articles and books gradually began to appear. One of the first important pieces on *The French Lieutenant's Woman* came from Elizabeth D. Rankin, who argued that Chapter 13, and other conspicuous interventions by the narrator, were in fact devices to ensure 'the literary acceptance (survival) of [Fowles's] actually quite conventional novel'. Rankin called this concealment 'cryptic colouration' (Rankin, 1973, 196), a Darwinian term defined by Fowles as 'survival by learning to blend with one's surroundings – with the unquestioned assumptions of one's age or social caste' (*FLW*, 143). Thus Rankin's argument was the opposite of that in Mary Conroy's review in *The Times*. The text's experimental features were not in fact signs of Fowles's failure to produce a proper novel, as Conroy thought, but 'a smokescreen, under cover of which [the narrator] intends to continue a quite traditional sort of narrative' (Rankin, 1973, 196). This tactic was devised so that *The French Lieutenant's Woman*'s didactic message about existentialism would be accepted by the very literary establishment that Fowles found so dismissive.

In her belief that the key to the novel was existential freedom, Rankin was in step with the views of other 1970s critics. William J. Palmer defined Charles's relationship with Sarah in terms of his 'movement through inner space to an existentialist destination in the world of light at the end of the tunnel' (Palmer, 1974, 94). Peter Wolfe placed Charles Smithson as a universal figure, who 'exists both in Victorian England and all time [. . .] he reflects all of us' (Wolfe, 1979, 142). Thus Wolfe turned the central existentialist dilemma of the male protagonist into that of *any* human seeking authentic individuality.

Fowles's retrospective interpretation of his own novel, nearly contemporary with Wolfe's, in the essay 'Hardy and the Hag' (1977), also universalized Charles Smithson's problems, but was built on a psychoanalytic approach, based on an article Fowles had read by the psychologist Gilbert J. Rose. Worryingly, for feminist readers, Fowles's interpretation was centred on the experience of the male novelist. He argued that the dual ending arose because he was torn between wanting to reward Charles '(my surrogate) with the woman he loved and wishing to deprive him of her' (*W*, 169). Thus Charles's existentialist choices were recast, by none other than his creator, as psychic dilemmas prompted by the inner compulsions shared by the male character and writer. Rose argued that the creative impulse of the novelist can be reduced to a means of negotiating the limits between the psyche and the world, and of compensating for the loss of the mother by 'creating [a world] of his own, peopled with products of self' (Rose, 1972, 174). Despite Fowles's positive account of Rose, *The French Lieutenant's Woman* is too complex to respond well to such psychoanalytical models. Sigmund Freud, as Frank Kermode observed, was

> given to analysing authors and artists rather than texts; he used the works as clinical data, or, at best, as evidence in support of his theory of cultural history as the phylogenetic parallel to what goes on in the individual psyche. (Kermode, 1983, 125)

According to Kermode, then, Freud was a closet Linnaean: he sought to classify authors according to their animalistic demonstration of species-wide, 'phylogenetic' instincts and drives. Fowles's novel, with its demonstration of a chaotic, Darwinian nature in perpetual flux, tends to resist such classification. Through devices such as Chapter 13, *The French Lieutenant's Woman* problematizes the Freudian focus on the author, rather than the text. By placing an authorial figure within the novel, who turns out to be 'just another character, though in a different category from the purely fictional ones' (*W*, 21), the text invites the reader to examine it *as* a text, and the narrator as part of the fiction, rather than to seek a psychologically transparent, readily analysable author situated conveniently above it.

Other early critics of the novel shied away from existentialism and psychoanalysis, and instead concentrated on the text's re-creation of the Victorian period and its status as a historical novel. Barry N. Olshen praised Fowles's 'quite considerable exercise of historical imagination' (Olshen, 1978, 64) in which 'The tension between fiction and reality and between the historical past and the present are manipulated from the first page to the last' (65). Robert Huffaker acknowledged that 'At its elementary level, *The French Lieutenant's Woman* is a magnificent historical novel' but argued that it was also 'far more' than this. He anticipated later postmodernist readings by claiming that the novel offered 'an original modern expansion upon older traditional forms'. 'Written both admiringly and ironically', it paid 'tribute to past techniques while gently spoofing them' (Huffaker, 1980, 98). Revealingly, Huffaker had trouble finding the right term for the novel's treatment of its Victorian sources: it was 'not purely parody or pastiche, terms implying some disrespect for the model; nor is such reworking simply imitation or emulation' (98). In the following decade, postmodernist readers would develop the debate initiated by Huffaker, by basing their accounts of the novel on its complex imitation of its source material.

POSTMODERNIST APPROACHES

In the late 1980s, critics began to read *The French Lieutenant's Woman* in terms of its postmodernist parody: or, to borrow a phrase from Fowles's *The Ebony Tower*, its paradoxical combination of 'a homage and a kind of thumbed nose to a very old tradition' (*ET*, 23). Linda Hutcheon claimed that *The French Lieutenant's Woman* was a historiographic metafiction, that is to say, a postmodernist novel that aspired to historical reference and yet also knew itself to *be* fiction, as it demonstrated that history, theory and the novel have a shared basis in narrative (see Chapter 1). Hutcheon identified *The French Lieutenant's*

Woman's relationship to its Victorian sources as one of parody, but lacking the mockery and assumption of superiority conventionally associated with the term. Instead, its parody was one of a number of self-reflexive devices: 'Its combined use of allegory, parody, self-mirroring structures and overt commentary make it a kind of summation of metafictional techniques' (Hutcheon, 1986, 118). Hutcheon showed how parody in the postmodernist period differed from its modernist ancestor, as found, for instance, in the poetry of T. S. Eliot, whose fragmented allusions to the canon in works such as *The Waste Land* concealed a 'wishful call to continuity'. Postmodernist parody, by contrast, 'paradoxically both incorporates and challenges that which it parodies' (Hutcheon, 1988, 11).

Following Hutcheon's work, there was considerable debate over how and why *The French Lieutenant's Woman* interpreted and reworked its historical sources. M. Keith Booker, for instance, believed that although Fowles parodied Victorian novels, he did not mock them. Instead,

> the force of Fowles's parody is an historical one – the difference between his text and the texts being parodied derives mostly from the simple fact that they were written in different centuries ruled, as Foucault might put it, by different epistemes. (Booker, 1991, 193)

Booker argued that *The French Lieutenant's Woman*'s parody was epistemological, because the novel and its sources were based on different frameworks for creating and organizing knowledge. Postmodernism is supposedly one such framework, as was the loosely 'Victorian' *episteme* which might be said to run from the Romantic period until the onset of modernism, straddling the long nineteenth century.

Other readers of *The French Lieutenant's Woman* avoided the term 'parody', even though they recognized the novel's widespread (and not always reverent) use of sources. Peter Conradi, for instance, preferred to call the novel a 'pastiche' of Victorian fiction (Conradi, 1982, 59, 62). The reason for his choice of this term is not clear. It is possible that he had in mind parody without comedy, and was thus in accord with Fredric Jameson's view that unlike parody, pastiche is 'amputated of the satiric impulse, devoid of laughter [. . .] Pastiche is thus blank parody, a statue with blind eyeballs' (Jameson, 1991, 17). According to Conradi, *The French Lieutenant's Woman* was indeed laughter-free: 'Fowles [is] a quite astonishingly unfunny writer' (Conradi, 1982, 105). However, Fowles's novel is wittier than the dour existentialist tome implied by Conradi: parts of it *are* motivated by 'the satiric impulse', or at least a wry sense of humour. To list some of Fowles's jokes: Mr Freeman suggests to Charles that Mr Darwin, because of his evolutionary theories, should be locked up in the monkey-house at the zoo (13); Charles falls asleep while Ernestina is reading aloud from a worthy but dull verse epic, *The Lady of La Garaye*, whereupon Ernestina literally throws the book at him (116); Ernestina compares the desiccated old ladies at a London society party to the geological specimens collected by Charles (83); when Sarah hands Charles two tests, or fossilized marine shells (137), the term implies a 'symbolic sexual comedy' (Palmer, 1974, 95), in which she has his testes in her hand; most memorably, the narrator sends Mrs Poulteney to hell in the false ending of Chapter 44, while she screams on her way down that Lady Cotton must be behind this (326). *The French Lieutenant's Woman* is not dominated by comedy, certainly, but it shows its awareness of the comic potential of seeing Victorian culture through a modern lens, without complacently asserting the superiority of the latter.

The problem remains of *why* the novel copies from the past with irony, but does not always ridicule it: is this because the novel is postmodernist, or is it in fact being quite traditional? According to the narrator, making irony conventional is a *Victorian* characteristic: Charles's 'negative but comfortable English soul – one part irony to one part convention' is cited as a reason for his failure to embrace Catholicism as a student (*FLW*, 20). Charles's sense of irony is 'a fundamental aspect of his psyche' (280). Ernestina, like Charles, has 'a very proper respect for convention' combined with 'a sense of self-irony' (33–4). One might almost say, in tongue-in-cheek counterpoint to Sarah's and Charles's anticipation of existentialism, that Ernestina and the early Charles (before he meets Sarah) are postmodernists before their time, as they understand their dependency on the traditions they have inherited but are prepared to treat them with ironic distance.

Such a comparison cannot be taken too seriously, but it does expose a problem with postmodernist readings of *The French Lieutenant's Woman*: they assume that the novel's ironic references to the past make it part of a distinct cultural movement or school belonging to the late twentieth century. Susana Onega, by contrast, has pointed out that by allowing an omniscient narrator to comment on material from the past, Fowles 'is drawing on a convention as old as the novel itself' (Onega, 1989, 69). Onega saw Chapter 13 as a major caesura within the text, a frame-breaking device that allowed the novel to *become* postmodernist: Fowles's text worked 'By starting as a Victorian novel and then developing from this into a post-Modernist metafictional parody of Victorian conventions' (91). Onega's reading implied that the novel exploited postmodernist parody just as it used Victorian realism, as a fictional stance to imitate and play with, and did not fully adopt either. Katherine Tarbox, another late 1980s critic, confirmed this, arguing that like other writers of 'the genre of the book-being-written', the narrator sets out 'to examine some of the specious assumptions novels and their readers make' (Tarbox, 1989, 81).

Tarbox compared Fowles not only to his experimental contemporaries Vladimir Nabokov and Alain Robbe-Grillet, but also to Laurence Sterne, writer of the playful, reflexive classic *The Life and Opinions of Tristram Shandy*, first published in 1759–67. This raises the question of how long experiments such as those of *The French Lieutenant's Woman* have been going on. Fowles's text may not be an experiment as such, but an exploration of the productive tension between experimentation and conservatism that has always informed the novelistic tradition. Lance St John Butler saw Fowles as having begun his career within an existentialist paradigm of freedom as 'an indispensable absolute', but to have been moving *towards* a poststructuralist sense of freedom as 'a chimera, an endlessly deferred goal' (Butler, 1991, 63). *The French Lieutenant's Woman* can be read as a stage of this process. In 'Notes on an Unfinished Novel', Fowles posed two important questions: 'To what extent am I being a coward by writing inside the old tradition? To what extent am I being panicked into avant-gardism?' (*W*, 18). As early as 1974, William J. Palmer pointed out that the juxtaposition of the two questions was no coincidence: it 'defines [Fowles's] real position and signals his quest for a middle ground between the two extremes' (Palmer, 1974, 4).

Postmodernist critics like Hutcheon would argue that to see Fowles's novel as a compromise between tradition and modernity is too simplistic: the text, regardless of its author's position, may signify something more complex and paradoxical than a search for a 'middle ground'. Readers will continue to debate whether *The French Lieutenant's Woman* is an exemplary postmodernist text, an existentialist one, or something else; but it may be useful to see it as a novel of transition, involving sometimes contradictory juxtapositions of the modernity of existentialism with the postmodernity of metafiction. Fredric Jameson has called 'the existential model of authenticity and inauthenticity [. . .] a casualty of the poststructural or postmodern period' (Jameson, 1991, 12). Jameson's metaphor implies the death of existentialism; Fowles's novel, by contrast, proposes a continuing debate between existentialism and postmodernism, by allowing both to combine, if not in harmony, at least in unresolved contradiction or Bakhtinian dialogue. As a result, the text cannot be read simply as historical, existentialist or postmodernist. It 'violates the rules of both history and fiction, and promotes its own world, which defies any fixed meaning or any form of classification' (Salami, 1992, 109).

ALTERNATIVE INTERPRETATIONS

In parallel with postmodernist readings, critics have paid attention to Fowles's treatments of gender, and have debated whether his works can be called feminist. Bruce Woodcock, in *Male Mythologies: John Fowles and Masculinity* (1984), suggested that the male figures in Fowles's novels are patriarchal. Woodcock pointed out that *The French Lieutenant's Woman* made the basic feminist statement that 'unless the species is ready to adapt to new social conditions, which include the emancipation of women', then some men may find themselves outpaced by evolution; however, against this must be set the 'highly ambiguous' viewpoint of the male narrator (81). Woodcock's thesis was that the novel charted 'the male anxiety of the late 1960s at a newly-emergent female autonomy' (82) and that therefore Sarah was ambiguously dramatized by the narrator as an image of Victorian and modern male anxieties about women, a figure designed to embody these anxieties but also to assuage them as part of a phallocentric sexual fantasy. In short, 'Sarah is *used* both to teach men a lesson about themselves and as an instrument for imaginary gratification' (108: emphasis in original). Pamela Cooper combined feminist and postmodernist approaches when she argued that Sarah is herself like a text, and that the novel 'explicitly asserts that ultimate fictionality which compromises her as a creator' (Cooper, 1991, 117). In effect, Sarah's unknowability and textuality reinforce the dominance of the narrator and, by implication, the novelist: by showing that she is a literary character, these male figures remain 'generators of any narrative truth which might seem to originate with her' (116). Cooper thus believed that Sarah's artistic power was denied, and the novel was ultimately patriarchal, despite its appearance of feminism.

More recently, in a reading influenced by queer theory, and lesbian accounts of fiction such as Judith Roof's *A Lure of Knowledge: Lesbian Sexuality and Theory* (Roof, 1993), David W. Landrum claimed that Sarah Woodruff's sexuality is ambiguous. The narrator seems to want to suppress any possibility of a lesbian interpretation of Sarah, but 'is never able to completely affirm Sarah's heterosexuality' (Landrum, 2000, 60). There are, as Landrum pointed out, two main references to lesbianism in the novel: Sarah's sharing a bed with the servant girl Millie at Mrs Poulteney's house, and Charles's fear that Sarah may be sexually involved with Christina Rossetti, who is living with her in London at the end of the novel. In each case homosexuality is denied (by the narrator and Charles respectively), but Sarah's sexuality remains inscrutable. Landrum queried the attribution of 'perversity' (*FLW*, 156) and 'enormity' (435) to the idea of Sarah as a lesbian, suggesting that the male narrator and character protest too much. Neither lesbian reference is necessary to the plot: they seem to be introduced only so that they can be rejected with conspicuous haste. Landrum's reading is an example of how *The French Lieutenant's Woman* is complex and multifaceted enough to allow critics to create interpretations directly contrary to the statements of the narrator.

A number of readers have offered their own interpretations of the novel based on distinctive theories or approaches. Carol M. Barnum, in a book revealingly entitled *The Fiction of John Fowles: A Myth for Our Time*, saw Fowles as a contemporary myth-maker, and connected the novel with Jungian archetypes. Sarah is 'an anima figure who will awaken in Charles the hidden side of himself' (Barnum, 1988, 53). Sarah also serves as the guide in his mythic quest, replacing 'the archetypal figure of the wise old man' (55). H. W. Fawkner, in *The Timescapes of John Fowles*, argued that 'Temporality is a master-key to Fowles's fiction' (Fawkner, 1984, 37). His study, derived from his reading of the psychology of time, argues that *The French Lieutenant's Woman* is based on a fundamental asymmetry between 'the long existential vistas in which *nothing* happens' and 'those minutes (sometimes seconds, sometimes hours) when *everything* happens' (30–1: emphasis in original). The novel 'catches the pattern of this existential rhythm' which, Fawkner argued, has been common to animals for hundreds of millions of years (31). Mythic or scientific readings such as those of Barnum and Fawkner developed the early existentialist and psychoanalytic readings of Rose, Olshen, Fowles and others, as they sought to universalize the novel and the author's creativity. Fittingly, given his own interest in psychology as expressed in 'Hardy and the Hag', Fowles wrote the Foreword to Fawkner's study, in which he stated it was one of the few critical works whose approach interested him personally (9).

Another new critical approach was developed in a collection of essays, *John Fowles and Nature: Fourteen Perspectives on Landscape* (Aubrey, ed., 1999), which brought together the work of scholars responding to Fowles's statement that his relationship with nature is the 'key' to his fiction (*T*, 35). Suzanne Ross interpreted *The French Lieutenant's Woman* through ecofeminism, which seeks to refigure the traditional relationships between women and nature, so that 'the whole system of oppositional and hierarchically ordered categories – culture *and* nature, man *and* woman – [can] itself be reconceived' (Ross, 1999,

182: emphasis in original). Fowles, she believed, was engaged in a similar project in *The French Lieutenant's Woman*, which overturned this 'dualistic conceptual system' to offer a new sense of human identity as *part of* nature (192). In an essay with similar concerns, Eileen Warburton argued that throughout Fowles's work runs 'the repeated pattern [. . .] of a dead and resurrected woman in an Edenic, primeval landscape' (Warburton, 1999, 123): Sarah's role, as a woman who appears to be a corpse at Carslake's Barn, but then springs to life, is to educate Charles to see the world around him as it really is, rather than through the lens of his patriarchal, Victorian prejudices (see Chapter 3). Carol M. Barnum argued that Fowles's art, 'With its emphasis on internal creativity and its concentration on the creative process', is designed to 'challenge us to seek the mystery of our own nature' (Barnum, 1999, 94). James R. Aubrey connected Fowles's interest in nature to his commitment to existentialism: natural landscape in his work is there 'to help enable a character, a writer, and a reader to attain heightened awareness of his or her freedom' (Aubrey, 1999, 24). This led Aubrey to read the Undercliff as 'a morally neutral landscape' (23) that is nevertheless politically and spiritually charged (see Chapter 3).

While it is impossible to comment on every single reading made of *The French Lieutenant's Woman*, it is clear that critics began by looking at what was most conspicuous in the text – that is, its experimental form, its historical focus and its concern with existential freedom. Around the 1980s, it became common to read the novel as an exemplary postmodernist text, whose playful reworking of its sources embodied the ironic but paradoxically reverent spirit of the mid to late twentieth century. Since then, approaches have diversified, supporting the suggestion that *The French Lieutenant's Woman* will continue to carry enough critical freight to become part of the canon, enjoyed by scholars and by a mass readership for some time to come.

REPUTATION AND FUTURE

The sad news of the death of John Fowles of heart failure aged 79 on 5 November 2005 caused the inevitable process of assessing his literary standing to begin. The obituaries published at the time, although acknowledging Fowles's decline in literary fashion since the 1970s, all lauded him for his oeuvre and singled out *The French Lieutenant's Woman* as the novel that would seal his reputation. Melvyn Bragg commented that *The French Lieutenant's Woman* would probably be read 'for some decades' and that many thought of it as Fowles's masterpiece (Bragg, 2005, 2–3). The *Daily Telegraph* also singled out *The French Lieutenant's Woman* for praise, commenting that it 'convincingly evoked the Victorian world with remarkable acuity' (unsigned, 2005, 21). The novel was appropriately placed in context by *The Times*, which argued that with it Fowles's reputation 'reached its zenith' (unsigned, 2005, 58). The novelist Sebastian Faulks pointed out that although unfashionable in the later decades of the twentieth century, 'Fowles was an original and exciting novelist when there were very few of those at work in Britain' (cited in Pook, 2005, 8). The consistent thread running through these immediate reactions to Fowles's death was that although his reputation had declined in the decades following its publication, *The French Lieutenant's Woman* would form the keystone of future re-evaluations of the novelist and his work.

The debate about Fowles intensified when his *Journals*, which he had kept from his early twenties onwards, were published in two volumes (Volume 1 in 2003, Volume 2 in 2006). Charles Drazin, the editor of both volumes, pointed out that Fowles had asked for the *Journals* to be cut to a publishable length but not censored (Drazin, 2003, xvii). Given Fowles's refusal to bowdlerize the *Journals*, it is not surprising that selected passages were taken by some reviewers as evidence of his alleged elitism and self-importance, which by implication devalued the novels. The most negative review came from Ian Sansom in the *London Review of Books*, who argued that the *Journals* revealed the 'profound self-love' of a writer who thought 'everybody else has a cramped little mind and lives in a cramped little house, and is useless, dead, pointless, ugly and stupid' (Sansom, 2004, 3). An early response to such comments came from Catherine Gander, who pointed out the reductiveness of separating the *Journals* from Fowles's experiments in fiction. She argued that they

contained, 'at the very least, lyrical embellishments of his attitudes and opinions, and, at the most, inventions of and experi-
mentations in authorial voice' (Gander, 2005, 28). After 1985,
when his last novel, *A Maggot*, was published, Fowles's output
shifted to essays, but this did not mean his writing had
become simply factual. Even in his later non-fiction, he was 'still
telling stories about the world and his position within it', arriv-
ing at truth through 'a voyage through a personal labyrinth'
(Stephenson, 2003, 72). Thus when Fowles refused to allow
potentially damaging remarks to be edited out of the *Journals*,
he might have wished to be true to a constantly evolving storytelling persona as much as to an essential self. Just as the narrator of *The French Lieutenant's Woman* is not Fowles himself, so
the writer of the *Journals* may be another literary creation.
Fowles knew that critics often mistook the written Fowles for the
writer, and found the situation frustrating: 'something called
"Fowles" has become my representative in the public world, a
kind of vulgar waxwork figure with (it seems to me) only a crude
caricature resemblance to the original' (*W*, 233). Such a fission of
the novelist's identity would not impress Sansom, who censured
Fowles for what he saw as the class bias, racism and sexism of the
Journals: '[Fowles] hates "the provincial", obviously, and he isn't
much keener on Jews, or foreigners [. . .] he spends a lot of time
writing about how much he despises his girlfriends' (Sansom,
2004, 4). There is a case to be answered here: perhaps Fowles's
personal attitudes were somewhat less free from the institutionalized snobbery, racism and chauvinism of mid-twentieth-
century Britain than his writing published at the time might have
suggested.

As Fowles argued in *The Aristos*, however, the dividing line
between the Many and the Few runs within individuals, not
between them (see Chapter 6). Whatever Fowles wrote in the
Journals that has since been read as insensitive, they reveal a per-
sonality capable of genuine insight. There are many striking passages on nature and on art. One such comes from his visit to the
Shaker Museum at Hancock in 1977, and clearly anticipates
A Maggot, Fowles's imaginary account of the conception and
birth of Ann Lee, founder of the Shakers (see Chapter 6):

The Shakers died of their own genius for perfection; of, at their best, very nearly achieving it. They were too good for this world, since evolution itself is mainly fuelled by faults.

Never mind: Hancock remains both rich and moving, a record of one of the strangest of all explorations by the human spirit. (*J II*, 240)

The last sentence might apply equally to Fowles's work. What matters, in the end, is what his writing achieved and continues to achieve: its evolution may perhaps have been 'fuelled by faults', but the ongoing record of Fowles's ideas remains 'rich and moving'. The continuing critical debate about *The French Lieutenant's Woman* is proof that Fowles, whatever his alleged personal failings, wrote enduring, complex fictions. Part of their complexity was not to reflect their creator in an egocentric way, but to obscure him and thus give autonomy to the reader. Fowles was, and remains, a writer 'with freedom [his] first principle, not authority' (*FLW*, 99).

DISCUSSION QUESTIONS

1. Fowles was dismissive of professional literary criticism, deriding 'literary influences and theories of fiction, all the rest of that purely intellectual midden which faculty hens and cocks so like scratching over' (*T*, 36). In your experience, have critical readings of *The French Lieutenant's Woman* been helpful? Why, or why not? Do you prefer the work of one critic over another? Why?

2. Compare your view of the novel's treatment of Sarah Woodruff to that suggested in feminist accounts, such as those by Pamela Cooper or Bruce Woodcock (see Bibliography below). Are these critics right to claim that the novel is basically patriarchal, despite the independence of its heroine?

CHAPTER 5

THE NOVEL ON FILM

By far the most important adaptation of Fowles's novel into another medium is the 1981 United Artists film directed by Karel Reisz and scripted by Harold Pinter, starring Meryl Streep as Sarah and Jeremy Irons as Charles. Not only was Reisz's movie a considerable achievement in its own right, but it also influenced later period adaptations which aimed to engage with twentieth- and twenty-first-century *images* of the past as much as real historical people and events. The final scene of Shekhar Kapur's *Elizabeth*, for instance, shows how Queen Elizabeth I asserts her sovereignty by literally making herself up into the image of Gloriana, The Virgin Queen. Before appearing in court, she has her ladies-in-waiting cut off most of her hair and apply white face paint to create a skin tone that is icy, aloof and like a death mask. She tells them, 'I have become a virgin'. She then announces to the court 'I am married to England', after having made her entrance dressed in silvery fabric, bewigged and bathed in symbolic white light (Kapur, 1998). The captions at the end of the picture announce that she reigned for another 40 years, by which time England was the richest and most powerful country in Europe. Like Sarah Woodruff, Kapur's Elizabeth is a woman who makes her destiny and determines to live by it, but whose self-determination is partly a modern construction, a necessity stemming from the demands of feminism and the existentialist idea that a person can create who they are. To gain what she wants, Elizabeth turns herself into a virgin, just as the virginal Sarah takes on the appearance of the French lieutenant's whore.

Like Reisz and Pinter, Kapur makes a historical heroine anticipate contemporary ideas of how women can reinvent themselves. Belén Vidal Villasur's comment on some recent period pictures, including *Elizabeth*, applies equally to Reisz's film:

> The iconography and narrative conventions deployed by these and other films both call forth and playfully betray a popular knowledge of the (European) past beyond the versions sanctioned by official history, and official literary history. These films are first and foremost symptomatic of the contemporary imagination, offering unfamiliar takes on familiar myths. (Villasur, 2002, 5)

By 1981, Fowles's text had become a bestseller and critical success, one of the 'familiar myths' that Pinter and Reisz set out to defamiliarize. In refusing to mimic the 'sanctioned' text or to be satisfied with the critical and popular perception of its strengths, the screenplay and film were transgressive. However, they were also faithful to the book on another level, by imitating the irony and freedom with which it dealt with 'the (European) past', and looked afresh at canonized literature in order to create an independent work of art.

THE MAKING OF THE FILM

Even before *The French Lieutenant's Woman* was published, Fowles and his editor Tom Maschler were thinking of how and by whom the novel might be adapted for cinema, and they asked Karel Reisz to direct. He refused, on the grounds that he had just made a difficult period film, *Isadora*. The process of getting a director contracted, the novel scripted, the film financed and actors cast was so long and complicated that Fowles reflected on it wryly as 'the filming, or more accurately the non-filming' of the book (*W*, 38). In all, the transition from novel to film took 12 years, and Fowles recalled that there were so many potential writers and directors involved at different times, all of whom had to leave the project for various reasons, that he became 'distinctly cynical' about the process (*W*, 38). Even after 1978, when Reisz agreed to work on the film, there were difficulties involved. Warner Brothers initially agreed to fund the project but withdrew in mid-January 1980, only four months before shooting was due to start, on the grounds that the proposed movie was 'an art film' and the allocated budget was too large for such a seemingly uncommercial project. Maschler, who had taken on the role of producer, called Warner Brothers and furiously asked, 'What do you want us to make [. . .]? A musical?' (Warburton, 2004, 401). In the end, Meryl Streep's agent arranged for United Artists to finance the project, and shooting could go ahead.

Fowles was not prepared to attempt the script. He had written the screenplay for the adaptation of *The Magus*, which turned out badly. In his own words, it was one of the worst films of the 1960s: 'disastrously awful' (*Con*, 66). Fortunately for *The French Lieutenant's Woman* project, Fowles and Maschler were eventually able to engage Harold Pinter as screenwriter. Pinter, unlike Fowles, was a theatre-trained minimalist, expert at 'reducing the long and complex without distortion' (*W*, 43). He was, of course, famous as a playwright. Moreover, he was able to work easily with Fowles and Karel Reisz. Fowles's essay, 'The Filming of *The French Lieutenant's Woman*', refers to the 'unusual sense of trust' he developed towards the screenwriter and director and their 'devotion, ingenuity, teamwork' (*W*, 47). Fowles' sole involvement with the script appears to have been to rewrite two scenes that called for a sense of romance: the proposal scene between Charles and Ernestina and the final scene between Sarah and Charles (Warburton, 2004, 399). Fowles revised the latter because of 'the need for emotion', which he felt Pinter's version lacked at that point: this was accepted by Pinter and Reisz, 'in a sprit of friendship and co-operation that must be rare in the cinema' (*J II*, 252).

Pinter's screenplay was a superb achievement – in Fowles's words, 'the blueprint [. . .] of a brilliant metaphor' for the novel (*W*, 43). Pinter retained the original story but deleted many peripheral scenes. He removed Fowles's narrator by substituting a modern framing narrative whose ironic parallels with the main Victorian plot imitated the postmodernist, reflexive games about storytelling and history that are such an important part of the original text. In Pinter's framing story, Mike and Anna are actors playing Charles and Sarah, in a film-within-a-film also entitled *The French Lieutenant's Woman*. Mike and Anna's relationship mirrors that of the Victorian protagonists, except that each affair ends differently: Charles and Sarah are reunited at the house of her patron (now an architect, rather than Rossetti), but Anna and Mike separate when she abandons him at the party held to celebrate the end of filming. Thus the framing device enabled Pinter to emulate the novel's ambiguous dual ending.

The filming of the screenplay eventually went ahead from May to October 1980, and was, according to Fowles, 'extraordinarily peaceful and unfraught; a model of how such things should be done' (*J II*, 254). On first seeing the final film, Fowles reacted with guarded approval:

> I think my main quarrel would be over the cutting, too sharp for my taste, not enough time to linger. [. . .] Fine performances from Jeremy and Meryl, some of the Undercliff photography beautiful; and many, if not quite all, of the jumps out of past into present work well. (*J II*, 254)

Fowles regretted Reisz's deletion of two scenes from the final cut: that between Charles and the London prostitute, and Charles's final scene with Grogan. In the latter, Pinter gave Charles the lines 'She is free. I am free also. She has given me this freedom. I shall embrace it' (*S*, 80). This succinct statement of the novel's existentialist premise was something Fowles was sad to lose, but he had already grown to accept that cinema was a form of 'communal art' (*J II*, 254).

SCENES FROM THE FILM

The opening of Reisz's movie deserves an extended commentary. The film begins abruptly with Anna and her make-up artist on camera. Seagulls on the soundtrack suggest that we are on the coast. We see only part of Anna's face in the mirror held up to her. An off-screen voice asks 'Are you ready, Anna?' and she turns and nods: again, the hood conceals most of her face. She adjusts her skirt, revealing petticoats and therefore the historical setting. The camera zooms out to reveal various film technicians and prop workers moving off-screen. The second shot begins with a clapperboard, on screen very briefly: the board declares that this is scene 32 of *The French Lieutenant's Woman* directed by K. Q. Rogers, with Joe Ainsley as the cameraman. One critic's immediate reaction, and probably that of many viewers, was to suspect 'a horrendous editing gaffe' (Tucker, 1996, 68 n.). The clapperboard tells us we are already in take 2: in an ironic nod to the novel, the film acknowledges that all this is being done for the second time. The clapperboard is pulled away to reveal a medium distance shot of Lyme Regis harbour in Victorian times, a moored sailing ship, wheeling seagulls, nets hanging off the Cobb, two locals tending braziers: all the cars, megaphones and other signs of modernity have been erased. The off-screen director calls 'Action!' and 'Drag' as Anna, still dressed as Sarah Woodruff in her black cloak, walks into the frame in the middle distance. As she moves, the credits appear. Thus the traditional introduction to a film, where the credits come before anything else, is subverted: we are *already* in a film, watching what seems to be unedited footage, when the credits reveal the existence of the main film, with Meryl Streep and Jeremy Irons, rather than Anna and Mike, as the stars, and Reisz as the director. The camera rises as Anna walks up the steps onto the top of the Cobb, then it pans to follow her as she walks the length of the breakwater to embrace the cannon-bollard at the end. This tracking shot, from clapperboard to bollard, lasts a remarkable one minute forty-two seconds, and follows Anna throughout, creating an intense focus on the main character. At the very end of the shot, the soundtrack's romantic theme for strings is over-dubbed with church bells, which carry us over to the next few shots of Lyme.

An immediate contrast is established, as the now static camera focuses on the main street of Lyme, along which a shepherd is driving sheep, people are selling vegetables at a stall in front of a bookseller's, and a fishwife off screen cries out 'new mackerel'. A poster advertises a lecture on the Indian Mutiny. There follow some relatively rapid cuts, with plenty of people in the frame, and movement in different directions. During these establishing shots of the Lyme community, we see Sam in the street, carrying a bunch of white flowers, and appearing to flirt with an adolescent girl next to a cannon pointing out to sea, suggesting an ironic phallic parallel to the cannon-bollard on which Sarah leans: Sam's blatant sexuality is more honest, in a way, than Sarah's romantic melancholia. Cut to Charles in his hotel room, wearing a paisley dressing gown, chipping away at a fossil and humming to himself. A magnifying glass, tools, and a glass of brandy appear on his desk. He pauses in his work, as if reflecting on something important, then opens his window and shouts for Sam. It seems that he has just made the decision to propose marriage to Ernestina, as he tells Sam to prepare the carriage for a visit to her. The sequence implies that Charles may have a hidden connection with Sarah: he is the only other character seen alone. The incongruity of his chipping away at a fossil in a hotel room early in the morning while everyone else is busy at work suggests a degree of eccentricity that he shares with the melancholy, self-isolated woman on the Cobb.

The following shots, covering Charles's journey to Aunt Tranter's house and leading up to his proposal to Ernestina, convey a strong increase in pace: the soundtrack music runs at a faster tempo, with a jaunty tune having replaced the slower, melancholy theme that accompanied Sarah's walk on the Cobb. The cuts between shots are made more rapidly than in the Lyme street scene, and there are several quick dialogues. For instance, when Mary knocks and enters Ernestina's room to tell her that Charles has come, Ernestina is not fully dressed, and rapidly decides with Mary that she will wear her pink dress, while already moving through the doorway to her bedroom to put it on. We cut to Charles, walking up and down agitatedly in front of Aunt Tranter, tapping his glove against his hand, unable to contain his tension. She points out that 'The conservatory . . . is a private place. Will that suit?' (*S*, 5). The verbal content of the novel, much reduced in the screenplay, is now minimal, in places non-existent, as the film, wholly appropriately for the medium, conveys its ideas mainly through editing, *mise en scene*, camera positioning and the soundtrack, and the dialogue tends to reinforce what the visual content of the scene has already conveyed. The proposal scene is preceded by several rapid shots of an agitated Charles finding his way to the conservatory, Ernestina moving towards him in her pink dress, and Sam and Mary hiding at the window to watch what is going on. Once the scene begins, there are several changes of point of view, but the dialogue is now more sustained, as an important element of the plot is introduced. Sam and Mary watch from behind a net curtain, providing an ironic counterpoint: when Charles and Ernestina hold hands chastely, Sam wryly comments 'He's home and dry' (*S*, 7) and Mary bursts into giggles.

Just as Charles and Ernestina embrace, we hear a ringing telephone, and cut to Mike, naked in a hotel bed. He blearily answers the phone, and the camera zooms out to reveal Anna lying beside him, half asleep. He tells her, with dry irony, 'You're late' (*S*, 8). The cut to the modern scene is jarring for the audience, creating a deliberate disturbance of continuity that recalls the opening shots, where it was established that the Victorian scenes were part of a film. We jump from betrothal to adultery, from chastity to carnality, from Victorian dutifulness to modern cynicism. Anna comments, as Mike embraces her, 'Christ, look at the time. [. . .] They'll fire me for immorality [. . .] They'll think I'm a whore' (*S*, 9), a mocking reference to stereotypical Victorian values. Mike's reply is 'You are' (*S*, 9). While intended as a joke, this hints that Anna's distance from her role as the French lieutenant's whore, and Mike's from his as Charles, may not be as complete as the actors would like to think. This distance tends to narrow throughout the film, as the actors become increasingly identified with their roles, and their sense of knowing irony is eroded by anxiety about the consequences of their affair. This culminates in the final scene where Mike confusedly calls 'Sarah!' out of an upstairs window as Anna is driving away, implying he is in love with the character as much as the actress (*S*, 104). This makes explicit the blurring of the modern and Victorian time frames that has been going on throughout the film. The cinema audience knows that the joyful, reunited Charles and Sarah are part of a film, their love mere footage, a recording of a script. And so, for that matter, is Mike's affair with Anna. It isn't hard for the viewer to realize the implication that their own existence might be considered on the same basis. Pinter and Reisz successfully remind the audience of how artificial *their* lives are, with the pressures of history, ideology, psychology and social convention forming the script of their lives. The Victorian narrative, the modern frame and the lives of the audience

> merge, to remind us again of the fragile and ambiguous boundaries distinguishing our own realities, which, if we heed the screenplay, seem increasingly illusionary. (Tucker, 1996, 67)

THE NOVEL'S CINEMATIC QUALITIES

Even on the page, *The French Lieutenant's Woman* shows that it is visually as well as verbally conceived. On the Cobb, when they first meet, Sarah returns Charles's look with a powerful stare:

> Again and again, afterwards, Charles thought of that look as a lance; and to think so is of course not merely to describe an object but the effect it has. He felt himself in that brief instant an unjust enemy; both pierced and deservedly diminished. (16)

This is a female appropriation of the traditional male right to be the viewer, assessor or voyeur: or, in terms of film criticism, to own the gaze. The male gaze has been a key topic in cinema theory since Laura Mulvey's essay 'Visual Pleasure in Narrative Cinema', published six years after *The French Lieutenant's Woman*. Mulvey argued that:

> As the spectator identifies with the main male protagonist, he projects his look on to that of his like, his screen surrogate, so that the power of the male protagonist as he controls events coincides with the active power of the erotic look, both giving a satisfying sense of omnipotence. [. . .] The male protagonist is free to command the stage, a stage of spatial illusion in which he articulates the look and creates the action. (Mulvey, 1975, 12–13)

Mulvey claims that the male gaze of the protagonist is also that of the implied viewer, and that both are left in control of the visual stage at the expense of the female, who remains 'the silent image of woman still tied to her place as bearer of meaning, not maker of meaning' (7). On first reading, Sarah's silence on the Cobb in the opening chapters might seem to place her as such an objectified figure, pregnant with meaning but voiceless. This would make the novel a proto-cinematic patriarchal text that surrenders the gaze to Charles and thus to a reader who, like Mulvey's viewer, is tacitly assumed to be male. However, Sarah's return of Charles's gaze is far too powerful to permit this. Instead, *he* is the one under observation, 'pierced' by the 'lance' of Sarah's stare. The metaphor suggests not only the knightly weapon of romance, but also a lancet or scalpel. Moreover, it has phallic connotations, implying both penetration and desire, giving Sarah the forceful, dominant quality traditionally associated with the male in patriarchal accounts of sexuality.

Thus even before the film was made, Fowles's novel challenged the patriarchal conventions of viewing and looking that Mulvey describes. Pinter's screenplay retains this incident, with the direction, '*She turns sharply, stares at him. He stops speaking*' (S, 13: italics in original). It follows this with a close up of 'Sarah. Staring at him' (S, 13). Pinter presumably intends the female gaze to be directed at the viewer as well as at Charles, and to dominate the screen. This is altered somewhat in the film, where Sarah looks at Charles over three separate shots, interspersed with reaction shots of Charles looking at her. Though this appears to distribute the gaze evenly between the two protagonists, in fact the sequence suggests that Sarah retains control of the situation. The first shot begins simply with the back of her black hood, over Charles's call of 'Madam!'. Sarah turns and looks at him in surprise, then a wave crashes in front of the camera, blurring her face. The second shot has the camera zoom in gradually on her face as she looks first up, beyond and slightly above the camera, almost as if she is looking *past* Charles. She then focuses her gaze downward and narrows her eyes in a frank assessment of him. The third shot has her adjust her shawl over her shoulder and turn away. Thus Pinter's screenplay is developed by Reisz and

Meryl Streep to imply that Sarah does more than simply stare *at* Charles: she looks at the possibilities that lie within and beyond him, as a lover and potential rescuer (not from the storm on the Cobb, but from her situation in Lyme), then turns back to the sea, in a symbolic assertion of autonomy.

Fowles's novel treats the gaze in a way that seems designed for cinematic interpretation both by the reader and by a hypothetical future director, though the screenplay and film do not follow up every opportunity offered by the book. For example, in the novel, during a tea party at the bigoted Mrs Poulteney's house, a tense exchange of remarks about Sam and Mary's flirtation causes the ladies to avert their eyes, meaning that Charles and Sarah are at last able to exchange 'a look unseen' by the others: 'It was very brief, but it spoke worlds' (*FLW*, 106). There is a close parallel with the gazes of Sam and Mary, which meet and avoid each other 'by mutual accord' as they negotiate the terms of their relationship at Mary's employer's house, ironically at exactly the same time (107). Fowles's juxtaposition of parallel scenes based on the gaze, with minimal dialogue, invites cinematic treatment of the laconic sort preferred by Pinter. The screenplay, however, does not imitate this but leaves Sam and Mary out of the sequence, and glosses over the scene following the tense exchange with '*They all sip tea in silence*' (*S*, 35: italics in original). This creates a comic moment, but a historically complacent one, as the twentieth-century audience is encouraged to laugh at the characters' stiff, stereotypically Victorian embarrassment. In another stock element of drawing-room comedy, also used ironically, Pinter chooses to have Sarah slip Charles a note during the tea party scene. This, it turns out, invites him to an assignation in the local churchyard. There are clear cinematic reasons for this: it gives Reisz the chance to shoot a stormy mock-Gothic sequence by the church at night, scene 92 in the screenplay, where an organ peal bursts 'suddenly' from inside (*S*, 37) just as Sarah and Charles meet, creating an effective simulation of the novel's parodies of Victorian melodrama. The change of setting also avoids the visual repetition of constant return to the Undercliff.

Fowles, though, seems to have conceived the Undercliff trysts with the camera in mind. Charles's first, accidental meeting with

Sarah in the verdant wilderness, at the end of Chapter 10, suggests a cinematic sense of composition. Charles is given the opportunity to gaze on Sarah sleeping, reversing her visual penetration of him during the scene on the Cobb, but then she gazes back at him:

It was precisely then, as he craned sideways down, that she awoke.
She looked up at once, so quickly that his step back was in vain. (75)

This scene is based on mutual visual contact. There is no dialogue, apart from Charles's 'A thousand apologies. I came upon you inadvertently' (75): this relative silence suggests a cinematic imagination at work. The narrator's metaphor for Charles's shift of vocabulary according to his situation is '*cryptic coloration*, survival by learning to blend with one's surroundings', a biological image that is also one of sight (143: emphasis in original). When he meets Sarah on the Undercliff, her threat to his chameleon-like role-playing comes not so much from her verbal challenge to him as from her look, which suggests more than she can say: 'Though direct, it was a timid look. Yet behind it lay a very modern phrase: Come clean, Charles, come clean' (143). Fowles saw that his protagonists were, in a sense, film actors, who expressed themselves through appearance, gesture and the gaze as well as through words, and that his novel could create imaginative visual images, and thus, in effect, be screened in the reader's mind.

FOWLES AND CINEMA

As we saw in Chapter 1, *The French Lieutenant's Woman* 'started [. . .] as a visual image' of a woman on a deserted quay, one of the imaginary scenes, or 'mythopoeic "stills"' that often emerged unbidden from Fowles's mind (*W*, 14). Fowles's cinematic metaphor of 'stills' was no accident. He claimed to have seen a film every week since childhood (*W*, 23). In 1963, he wrote in his diary that that his second published novel, *The Magus*, was conceived in cinematic terms, 'not *of course* that I'm writing the book for the film of the book, but it's absurd to pretend that the cinema [. . .] can't influence one's writing deeply' (*J I*, 582: emphasis in original). In his notes written during the composition of *The French Lieutenant's Woman*, Fowles pointed out that he and all his contemporaries were deeply affected by the cinema not only as a medium to emulate, but also as a template for the imagination:

> How can so frequently repeated an experience [as cinema-going] not have indelibly stamped itself on the *mode* of imagination? At one time I analysed my dreams in detail; again and again I recalled purely cinematic effects: panning shots, close shots, tracking, jump cuts, and the rest. In short, this mode of imagining is far too deep in me to eradicate – and not only in me, but in all my generation. (*W*, 23–4: emphasis in original)

The main difference between the two media, which meant for Fowles that the novel was still in possession of 'a still-vast domain' inaccessible to the cinema (24), was not in composition, but in reception. He believed that the reader is far freer than the viewer to imagine what it is they see:

> The cinematic visual image is virtually the same for all who see it; it stamps out personal imagination, the response from individual *visual* memory. A sentence or paragraph in a novel will evoke a different image in each reader. This necessary cooperation between writer and reader – the one to suggest, the other to make concrete – is a privilege of *verbal* form; and the cinema can never usurp it. (*W*, 24: emphasis in original)

This view is intuitively appealing, but controversial. James Monaco puts forward the opposite argument, and, like Fowles, states it as bald fact:

> Novels are told by the author. We see and hear only what he wants us to see and hear. Films are more or less told by their authors, too, but we see and hear a great deal more than a director necessarily intends. (Monaco, 2000, 45)

Fowles and Monaco seem biased towards their respective media, as each suggests that one gives far more imaginative licence to its audience than the other. In fact, in *either* medium, the reader or viewer has a crucial role in determining meaning. This was suggested by Marshall McLuhan in 1964, in an account nearly contemporary with Fowles's novel:

> If the movie merges the mechanical and organic in a world of undulating forms, it also links with the technology of print. The reader in projecting words, as it were, has to follow the black and white sequences of stills that is typography, providing his own sound track. He tries to follow the contours of the author's mind at varying speeds and with various illusions of understanding. It would be difficult to exaggerate the bond between print and movie in terms of their power to generate fantasy in the viewer or reader. (McLuhan, 2001, 311)

Fowles was well aware of McLuhan and his then controversial ideas. When writing *The French Lieutenant's Woman*, he was reading Elizabeth Gaskell's *Mary Barton* (first published 1848), and noting how much more modern her dialogue sounded than his own. However, this did not deter him from writing, as at the same time he found himself influenced by McLuhan's view that literature is 'always a narrowing of the potential, a thin artifice compared to the full "nature" of all language' (*J II*, 27). McLuhan helped him gain confidence in the 'thin artifice' of his fake Victorian dialogue, which he devised to imitate a twentieth-century stereotype rather than a nineteenth-century reality:

> I am right to invent dialogue much more formal than the Victorians actually spoke. This gives the illusion better. In a sense an absolutely accurate Victorian dialogue would be *less* truthful than what I am doing. (*J II*, 27–8: emphasis in original)

In the novel, McLuhan is treated with deliberate flippancy. Sarah Woodruff possesses no books; the narrator points out that this is for financial reasons, and not because 'she was an early forerunner of the egregious McLuhan' (*FLW*, 41). McLuhan's claim, that the electric technology of film, TV, radio and related media would inevitably usurp the 'Gutenburg technology [of print], on and through which the American way of life was formed' (McLuhan, 2001, 19) is now a cliché, but was shockingly new in the 1960s. *The French Lieutenant's Woman* treats McLuhan with some degree of affection by using such a relatively refined expression of distaste as 'egregious', as if to point out how easily the print-based intellectual elite of the twentieth century could be shocked. This ironically makes the 1960s literary world rather like its own stereotype of the Victorian bourgeoisie, but with technology, rather than sexuality, as the main source of prudish aversion, and art, rather than religion, as the site of values that need to be defended even at the cost of embarrassment.

Despite the novel's playful acknowledgement of the coming of the new media (and of McLuhan as their prophet), Fowles's attitude to the commercial cinema mostly varied between indifference and contempt. In his introduction to Pinter's screenplay, which later became the essay 'The Filming of *The French Lieutenant's Woman*', he remarked:

> in a later novel, *Daniel Martin*, I did not hide the contempt I feel for many aspects of the commercial cinema [. . .] But for true cinema, conceived and executed by artists as an art, or at least as a craft by sincere craftsmen, I have always had the greatest liking and respect. (*W*, 44–5)

Fowles saw the work of Reisz, Pinter and the actors as 'true' cinema. The distinction he drew between this and the contemptible kind was not commercialization as such, but the placing of this above all other considerations. In fact, he saw film and the novel as 'much nearer sisters than anything else' (*W*, 45): 'the division we make between film and novel may be artificial' (*J II*, 76). Even when composing the novel, Fowles was, in fact, very much aware of the possibilities inherent in cinema, both as a medium of adaptation and as an influence on the visual imagination of novelist and reader.

DISCUSSION QUESTIONS

1. How important is it that Charles is a writer? Is it significant that Sarah ends up *among* writers (the Rossettis) but does not become one? By contrast, in the film, Pinter and Reisz made Sarah a gifted artist. Why might they have done this?
2. In the film, Harold Pinter's modern framing narrative introduced contemporary lovers whose lives paralleled those of the Victorian central couple. This structure was followed by A. S. Byatt in *Possession*. Does Pinter's idea improve the novel or detract from it? Why was it introduced? Overall, does the film compare well with the book?

CHAPTER 6

FURTHER READING

FICTION BY FOWLES

In retrospect, it can be seen how Fowles's previous writing had laid the foundations for his most critically and commercially successful work. Before *The French Lieutenant's Woman*, Fowles had published two novels, *The Collector* (1963) and *The Magus* (1965: revised 1977). *The Collector* anticipates *The French Lieutenant's Woman* in that it is based on the encounter of a man and woman from different social worlds: an inarticulate council worker kidnaps a talented, beautiful art student. Fowles intended the novel as an allegory of what he called the relationship between the Many and the Few (or the *hoi polloi* and the *aristoi*), meaning the tendency in society (and *within*, as well as between, individuals) for conformity, ignorance, cowardice and self-interest to dominate independence, knowledge, courage and selflessness. The member of the Few cannot always be such, as 'We are all sometimes of the Many. But he will avoid membership' as he seeks 'to be a free force in a world of tied forces' (*A*, 201).

The Magus, a longer and more elaborate novel than *The Collector*, is set on Phraxos, a fictional Greek island based on Spetsai, where Fowles worked as an English teacher from 1951 to 1953. Nicholas Urfe, the protagonist, is drawn into the orbit of a mysterious rich intellectual, Maurice Conchis, the magus of the title. Sarah Woodruff in *The French Lieutenant's Woman* amalgamates some of the features of Conchis and his two assistants, Lily and Rose. When drafting *The Magus*, Fowles had experimented with the idea of making Conchis a woman, but this proved technically difficult (*Con*, 125; *M*, 6–7): Sarah is the female magus that Fowles had wanted for the earlier novel. However, *The French Lieutenant's Woman* distances itself from *The Magus* by avoiding the rococo implausibility created by Conchis's elaborate, expensive and always perfectly arranged meta-theatrical games.

The Ebony Tower (1974), originally entitled *Variations*, is a collection of short stories that rework some of the situations of *The French Lieutenant's Woman*. In the title story, David Williams, a young painter, finds himself entranced by Diana, the assistant to an older artist. The setting in the Breton forest recalls the Arthurian legends and the Undercliff. In the same volume, Fowles translated *Eliduc*, one of the *Lais* of Marie de France, acknowledging his continuing debt to medieval romance (see Chapter 1). In 'The Cloud', a depressed woman feels cut off from the society around her, much like the melancholic Sarah Woodruff. Again, the setting is a French forest.

A Maggot (1985) was Fowles's second historical fiction, and the last novel he published during his lifetime. Set in 1736, it is the story of Rebecca Hocknell, a London prostitute who tries to break away from the patriarchal society around her. Unlike Charles and Sarah, Rebecca is not a self-centred existentialist. She ends the novel by giving birth to someone more important than she is: Ann Lee, the woman who in real history founded the Shakers, a feminist, pacifist religious movement. *A Maggot* retains the technical experimentation of *The French Lieutenant's Woman*, as it is nearly all in the form of the depositions of various witnesses, including Rebecca herself, written in question-and-answer form. The depositions reveal two versions of the central events: in a deliberately unstable structure that echoes the dual ending of *The French Lieutenant's Woman*, neither is allowed to become true. *A Maggot*'s shift away from the existentialist focus of the earlier novel suggests that to Fowles *The French Lieutenant's Woman* was not a definitive piece that he tried vainly to emulate, but a step in an ongoing literary journey, whose progress allowed for the questioning, and even repudiation, of the successful moves made before.

NON-FICTION BY FOWLES

Fowles followed *The Collector* with another, very different expression of his personal philosophy, *The Aristos* (1964), which is not a novel at all, because 'I did not intend to walk into the cage labelled "novelist" ' (*A*, 7). *The Aristos* appears totally unlike *The French Lieutenant's Woman* because it eschews any narrative, or attractive style, in order to function as a bald statement of its author's ideas. Despite their total difference in form, the two texts have similarities in content. For instance, *The Aristos* discusses 'sex's meteoric advent from behind the curtains and crinolines of Victorian modesty and propriety' (*A*, 158) and the need for less commercialization of sexuality and more education about it in contemporary society. Here, five years before *The French Lieutenant's Woman*, Fowles was questioning the modern age's belief that it is more sexually liberated than the nineteenth century because of its relative openness about the subject.

The Tree (1979) is Fowles's most significant piece on ecology. It makes many connections between creativity, psychology and nature. One of Fowles's favourite metaphors for literary composition, explored in *The Tree*, was that of a retreat into an unknown wood that was not only linked to the forests of medieval romance, but was also a psychological space. Fowles used a particular wooded dell near Lyme Regis to act as an imaginative backdrop for some of the meetings between Charles and Sarah in the Undercliff of *The French Lieutenant's Woman* because 'in a story of self-liberation, [these scenes] could have no other setting' (*T*, 79).

Islands (1978) is a long essay on landscape, designed to accompany photographs of the Scilly Isles, that becomes an extended meditation on the creative process. Fowles addresses the metaphorical relationship between literary composition and the sea voyage (see Chapter 1): 'I have always thought of my own novels as islands, or as islanded', because the island is where 'the magic' of unplanned discovery takes place (*I*, 30).

Wormholes: Essays and Occasional Writings, edited by Jan Relf (1998), is an essential collection of Fowles's most important essays, except *The Tree*. It includes *Islands* in abridged form, plus the essays most relevant to *The French Lieutenant's Woman*:

'Notes on an Unfinished Novel', 'The Filming of *The French Lieutenant's Woman*' and 'Hardy and the Hag'.

VICTORIAN TEXTS

The following nineteenth-century texts are worth studying in detail for their connections to *The French Lieutenant's Woman*.

Matthew Arnold, especially 'To Marguerite' (1853, 1857), *Culture and Anarchy* (1869).

Jane Austen, *Persuasion* (1818), particularly the chapters set in Lyme Regis.

Arthur Hugh Clough, whose poems are cited in several of Fowles's epigraphs.

Charles Darwin, *The Origin of Species* (1859), *The Descent of Man* (1871).

Gustave Flaubert, *Madame Bovary* (1857).

Thomas Hardy, especially *Tess of the D'Urbervilles* (1891), *The Well-Beloved* (1892), *A Pair of Blue Eyes* (1873). Several of Hardy's poems are quoted in the epigraphs to *The French Lieutenant's Woman*.

Karl Marx, *The Communist Manifesto* (1848), *Capital* (1867).

E. Royston Pyke (ed), *Human Documents of the Victorian Golden Age* (1967). Not a Victorian text as such, this is the anthology used by Fowles to research the novel. It is a compilation of excerpts from often marginal Victorian writing, exploring a wide range of fields, styles and themes.

Alfred Lord Tennyson, *In Memoriam* (1850), *Maud* (1855).

CONTEMPORARY FICTION

There are a number of recent novels that share some of the concerns of *The French Lieutenant's Woman* and bear comparison with it. There is only space here to touch on a few examples. Other historical fictions worth studying in the light of Fowles's work include: Peter Ackroyd, *Hawksmoor* (1985) and *Chatterton* (1987); Julian Barnes, *A History of the World in 10½ Chapters* (1989); Lawrence Norfolk, *Lemprière's Dictionary* (1991); Jeanette Winterson, *The Passion* (1987) and Sarah Waters, *Tipping the Velvet* (1988).

Pat Barker, *Regeneration* (1991). This is the first and best in Barker's trilogy of novels about the First World War. Some of the male protagonists are 'real' historical people: the poets Siegfried Sassoon and Wilfred Owen, and the psychologist W. H. R. Rivers (there is a parallel here with Fowles's use of the Rossettis). Barker's woman protagonist, Sarah Lumb, is economically and sexually liberated by the war, whereas the men are forced to confront horrors which expose their own impotence in the face of history. Rivers is a complex character, accepting Sassoon's homosexuality, and using what was then groundbreaking Freudian theory to cure traumatized officers only to send them back to their deaths at the front. Like Fowles, Barker sets her novel in the past in order to explore the impact of history upon psychology, gender, sexuality and identity.

Julian Barnes, *Flaubert's Parrot* (1984). Barnes's fake biography is narrated by a retired modern doctor trying to find the stuffed parrot once owned by the nineteenth-century French novelist Gustave Flaubert, author of *Madame Bovary* (a novel prosecuted as obscene because of its references to adultery, and read by Charles in private in *The French Lieutenant's Woman*). The doctor's search for the parrot is a metaphor for his obsessive quest to find the 'real' Flaubert and thus explain his own life. Barnes's sophisticated examination of authorship and the twentieth century's relationship to Victorian literature makes it very relevant to Fowles's work.

A. S. Byatt, *Possession* (1990: winner of the Booker Prize). Two modern academics pursue hidden biographical facts about two Victorian poets. The modern and Victorian pairs each become lovers, and it is finally revealed that one of the academics is the direct descendant of both Victorians. Byatt accurately imitates Victorian poetry and modern literary theory: her parody of the former is generous, of the latter satirical. Byatt avoids the tricksy narrator-novelist persona favoured by Fowles, instead using an unironic third-person perspective that in places assumes Victorian omniscience. Her structure allows the Victorian writers a great deal of space for their own work, which is quoted extensively (though actually invented by Byatt). *Possession* avoids Fowles's ambiguous dual ending, preferring a closed conclusion for the modern couple, supplemented by a postscript that resolves the Victorian plot.

J. G. Farrell, *The Siege of Krishnapur* (1973: winner of the Booker Prize). Along with Fowles's work, Farrell's remains one of twentieth-century British fiction's most celebrated Victorian historical novels. Farrell's great subject is the British Empire and its decline, chronicled also in *Troubles* (1970) and *The Singapore Grip* (1978). It is worth comparing Farrell's Lucy Hughes, a daring, liberated woman, to Sarah Woodruff, but the main connection between the novels is the irony with which they view their Victorian subject matter.

William Golding, *To the Ends of the Earth: A Sea Trilogy* (1980–9: one-volume edition 1991). The *Trilogy* was originally published as three separate novels, of which the first, *Rites of Passage*, won the Booker Prize in 1980. The *Trilogy* is the story of a young nobleman's voyage to Australia in the early nineteenth century. Like Fowles, Golding uses a romance plot, as the protagonist meets the love of his life in another ship, and they are separated by the sea, only to be reunited in the final volume. In an inversion of *The French Lieutenant's Woman*'s structure of existentialist protagonists fighting against a hostile world, Golding allows many of the *minor* characters to struggle to determine their political, social and sexual destinies but filters these conflicts through the eyes of a protagonist whose naivety, conservatism and privileged position mean that the reader has to infer much of what happens.

Graham Swift, *Waterland* (1983). A teacher of modern history tries to explain the French Revolution to a group of sixth-formers. He has his own personal history to tell, involving disastrous sexual experimentation. Swift interrupts and decentres these narratives with others: for example, the natural history of the eel, which implies an evolutionary, sexual core that determines human behaviour, in a manner comparable to *The French Lieutenant's Woman*'s use of Darwin as a context for the protagonists' existentialism. The novel is set against the flat background of the Fens, a monotonous and oppressive landscape that stands in direct contrast to Fowles's Undercliff.

Adam Thorpe, *Ulverton* (1992). This novel tells the story of a village in South West England from 1650 to 1988, with each chapter set in a separate period. In its regional setting and blending of historical perspectives, *Ulverton* resembles Fowles's work, and Fowles himself called it the most interesting first novel he had read in years (*G*). Like *The French Lieutenant's Woman*, it asks the reader to make direct connections between the contemporary world and earlier periods, which do not always show modernity in a favourable light.

CRITICISM AND THEORY

Many of the essential critical works on Fowles have been referred to already, especially in Chapter 4 (see also the Bibliography below). To begin reading about postmodernism, see Peter Brooker (ed), *Modernism/Postmodernism* (London: Longman, 1992); Patricia Waugh (ed), *Postmodernism: A Reader* (London: Arnold, 1992); and Tim Woods, *Beginning Postmodernism* (Manchester: Manchester University Press, 1999). Linda Hutcheon, in *A Poetics of Postmodernism* (London: Routledge, 1988), integrates *The French Lieutenant's Woman* into a wider theory. For a more complex but foundational text on postmodernism, see Jean-François Lyotard, *The Postmodern Condition: A Report on Knowledge*, translated by Geoff Bennington and Brian Massumi, foreword by Fredric Jameson (Manchester: Manchester University Press, 1984). For introductions to existentialism, see Jean-Paul Sartre and Philip Mairet, *Existentialism and Humanism* (London: Methuen, 1974), or Thomas Flynn, *Existentialism: A Very Short Introduction* (Oxford: Oxford University Press, 2006). For examples of the critical theory referred to in the novel, see Roland Barthes, *Image-Music-Text* (London: Fontana, 1977); Alain Robbe-Grillet, *For a New Novel* (New York: Grove Press, 1982); and Marshall McLuhan, *Understanding Media* (London: Routledge, 2001). An essential, if complex, text on modern and Victorian sexuality is Michel Foucault, *The History of Sexuality, Volume One: An Introduction* (Harmondsworth: Penguin, 1990). For a once groundbreaking but now more traditional view, see Sigmund Freud, *The Complete Introductory Lectures on Psychoanalysis* (London: George Allen & Unwin, 1971).

Website
http://www.fowlesbooks.com/index.htm   This is the only website dedicated to Fowles, and contains a biography, obituary, news of references to Fowles in the media, plus synopses of the novels, and plenty of useful links to other sites.

BIBLIOGRAPHY

Works by John Fowles
Fiction and poetry
(1963) *The Collector*. London: Jonathan Cape.
(1965) *The Magus*. Boston: Little, Brown.
(1969) *The French Lieutenant's Woman*. London: Jonathan Cape.
(1973) *Poems*. New York: Ecco Press.
(1974a) *The Ebony Tower*. London: Jonathan Cape.
(1977a) *The Magus: A Revised Version*. London: Jonathan Cape.
(1977b) *Daniel Martin*. London: Jonathan Cape.
(1982) *Mantissa*. London: Jonathan Cape.
(1985) *A Maggot*. London: Jonathan Cape.
(1996a) *The French Lieutenant's Woman*. London: Vintage.
(1996b) *A Maggot*. London: Vintage.
(1997a) *The Ebony Tower*. London: Vintage.
(1997b) *The Magus: A Revised Version*. London: Vintage.
(1998a) *The Collector*. London: Vintage.
(1998b) *Daniel Martin*. London: Vintage.

Non-fiction and translations
(1964) *The Aristos: A Self-Portrait in Ideas*. London: Jonathan Cape.
(1974b) Perrault, Charles, *Cinderella*. Translated by John Fowles. Illustrated by Sheilah Beckett. London: Jonathan Cape.

(1974c) *Shipwreck*. Photographs by the Gibsons of Scilly. London: Jonathan Cape.

(1978a) *Islands*. Photographs by Fay Godwin. London: Jonathan Cape.

(1978b) *Steep Holm – A Case History In The Study Of Evolution*. Co-author Rodney Legg. Sherborne, Dorset: Kenneth Allsop Memorial Trust.

(1979) *The Tree*. Preface and photographs by Frank Horvat. London: Aurum Press.

(1980) *The Enigma of Stonehenge*. Co-author Barry Brukoff. London: Jonathan Cape.

(1981a) *The Aristos* (revised edition). London: Triad Grafton.

(1981b) *A Brief History of Lyme*. Lyme Regis: Friends of the Museum.

(1990) 'Past and Present Comment: An Afterword', in Mick Gidley and Kate Bowles (eds), *Locating the Shakers*. Exeter: Exeter University Press, pp. 146–50.

(1992) 'Thank the gods for bloody mindedness'. *Guardian*, 28 May: 25.

(1994) De Duras, Claire, *Ourika, An English Translation*. Translated and foreword by John Fowles. New York: Modern Language Association.

(1998c) *Wormholes: Essays and Occasional Writings*. Ed. Jan Relf. London: Jonathan Cape.

(1999a) *Wormholes: Essays and Occasional Writings*. Ed. Jan Relf. London: Vintage.

(1999b) *Conversations with John Fowles*. Ed. Dianne L. Vipond. Jackson, MS: University Press of Mississippi.

(2000) *The Tree*. London: Vintage.

(2003) *The Journals, Volume 1*. Ed. Charles Drazin. London: Jonathan Cape.

(2006) *The Journals, Volume 2*. Ed. Charles Drazin. London: Jonathan Cape.

Film and television adaptations

Green, Guy (dir.) (1968) *The Magus*. 20th Century Fox. Starring Michael Caine, Anthony Quinn, Candice Bergen. Screenplay by John Fowles.

Knights, Robert (dir.) (1984) *The Ebony Tower*. Granada Television. Starring Laurence Olivier, Roger Rees, Gretta Scacchi. Screenplay by John Mortimer.
Reisz, Karel (dir.) (1981) *The French Lieutenant's Woman*. United Artists. Starring Meryl Streep, Jeremy Irons. Screenplay by Harold Pinter.
Wyler, William (dir.) (1965) *The Collector*. Columbia Pictures. Starring Samantha Eggar, Terence Stamp. Screenplay by Stanley Mann and John Kohn.

Secondary works
Reviews
Berridge, Elizabeth (1969) 'Recent Fiction'. *Daily Telegraph*, 12 June: 22.
Boston, Richard (1969) 'John Fowles, Alone But Not Lonely'. *New York Times Book Review*, 9 November: 2–3.
Chase, Edward T. (1969) 'Delectable Novel'. *New Republic*, 15 November: 23–4.
Conroy, Mary (1969) 'A novelist on the knowledge'. *Times*, 14 June: 22.
Davenport, Guy (1969) 'Lulu in Bombazeen'. *National Review*, 2 December: 1223, 1225–6.
Jones, D. A. N. (1969) 'Victorian Author'. *Times Literary Supplement*, 12 June: 629.
Lehmann-Haupt, Christopher (1969) 'On the Third Try, John Fowles Connects'. *New York Times*, 10 November: 45.
Mason, Michael (1981) 'Good Fiction and Bad History'. *Times Literary Supplement*, 27 November: 1391.
McDowell, Frederick P. W. (1970) 'Recent British Fiction: Some Established Writers'. *Contemporary Literature*, 11:3, (Summer): 401–31.
Mullan, John (2004) 'The man behind *The Magus*'. *Guardian*, 12 June, *G2*: 13.
Price, James (1969) 'Self-Dependence'. *New Statesman*, 13 June: 850.
Ricks, Christopher (1970) 'The Unignorable Real'. *New York Review of Books*, 14:3, 12 February, n. p.

Sansom, Ian (2004) 'His Own Peak'. *London Review of Books*, 26:9 (May). http://www.lrb.co.uk/v26/n09/print/sans01_.html Accessed 21.12.2005.

Trevor, William (1969) 'Conjuring with Ghosts'. *Guardian*, 12 June: 9.

Unsigned (1969) 'Imminent Victorians'. *Time*, 7 November: 108.

Wall, Stephen (1969) 'In Hardy's Foosteps'. *Observer*, 15 June: 29.

Watt, Ian (1969) 'A traditional novel? Yes, and yet . . .'. *New York Times Book Review*, 9 November: 1, 74.

Obituaries

Bragg, Melvyn (2005) 'John Fowles will be missed'. *Guardian*, 8 November: *G2*: 2–3.

Brown, Jonathan (2005) 'John Fowles, playful postmodernist who wrote *The French Lieutenant's Woman*, dies aged 79'. *Independent*, 8 November: 5.

Ezard, John (2005) 'John Fowles: Bestselling novelist who explored dark themes of time, power and relationships'. *Guardian*, 8 November: 36.

Higgins, Charles (2005) 'Reclusive novelist John Fowles dies at 79'. *Guardian*, 8 November: 5.

Pook, Sally (2005) 'Master novelist with an eye on immortality'. *Daily Telegraph*, 8 November: 8.

Unsigned (2005) 'John Fowles: Author whose skilful and cultured fictions were crowned by the commercial success of *The French Lieutenant's Woman*'. *Times*, 8 November: 58.

Unsigned (2005) 'John Fowles: Virtuoso author of *The Collector, The Magus* and *The French Lieutenant's Woman*'. *Independent*, 8 November: 58.

Unsigned (2005) 'John Fowles: Author of *The French Lieutenant's Woman* who explored the existential freedom of the individual'. *Daily Telegraph*, 8 November: 21.

Criticism about Fowles

Acheson, James (1998) *John Fowles*. London: Macmillan.

Aubrey, James R. (1991) *John Fowles: A Reference Companion*. New York, Westport, London: Greenwood Press.

Aubrey, James R. (1999) 'Introduction', in James R. Aubrey (ed.), *John Fowles and Nature: Fourteen Perspectives on Landscape*. London: Associated University Presses, pp. 13–43.

Barnum, Carol M. (1988) *The Fiction of John Fowles: A Myth for Our Time*. Greenwood, FL: Penkevill.

Barnum, Carol M. (1999) 'The Nature of John Fowles', in James R. Aubrey (ed.), *John Fowles and Nature: Fourteen Perspectives on Landscape*. London: Associated University Presses, pp. 87–95.

Booker, M. Keith (1991) 'What We Have instead of God: Sexuality, Textuality and Infinity in *The French Lieutenant's Woman*'. *Novel*, 23–24 (Winter): 178–97.

Bradbury, Malcolm (1987) 'The Novelist as Impresario: The Fiction of John Fowles', in Malcolm Bradbury, *No, Not Bloomsbury*. London: Andre Deutsch, pp. 279–93.

Butler, Lance St John (1991) 'John Fowles and the Fiction of Freedom', in James Acheson (ed.), *The British and Irish Novel Since 1960*. London: Macmillan, pp. 62–77.

Conradi, Peter (1982) *John Fowles*. London: Methuen.

Cooper, Pamela (1991) *The Fictions of John Fowles: Power, Creativity, Femininity*. Ottawa, Paris: University of Ottawa Press.

Drazin, Charles (2003) Introduction to John Fowles, *The Journals, Volume 1*. London: Jonathan Cape, pp. ix–xx.

Fawkner, H. W. (1984) *The Timescapes of John Fowles*. London: Associated University Presses.

Gander, Catherine (2005) 'Death of the author, not'. *Guardian*, 28 November: 28.

Huffaker, Robert (1980) *John Fowles*. Boston, MA: Twayne.

Hutcheon, Linda (1986) 'The "Real World(s)"' of Fiction: *The French Lieutenant's Woman*', in Ellen Pifer (ed.), *Critical Essays on John Fowles*. Boston, MA: G. K. Hall, pp. 118–32.

Jackson, Tony E. (1997) 'Charles and the Hopeful Monster: Postmodern Evolutionary Theory in *The French Lieutenant's Woman*'. *Twentieth Century Literature*, 43:2 (Summer): 221–42.

Kadish, Doris Y. (1997) 'Rewriting Women's Stories: *Ourika* and *The French Lieutenant's Woman*'. *South Atlantic Review*, 62:2 (Spring): 74–87.

Landrum, David W. (1996) 'Rewriting Marx: Emancipation and Restoration in *The French Lieutenant's Woman*'. *Twentieth Century Literature*, 42:1 (Spring): 103–13.

Landrum, David W. (2000) 'Sarah and Sappho: Lesbian Reference in *The French Lieutenant's Woman*'. *Mosaic*, 33:1 (March): 59–76.

Loveday, Simon (1985) *The Romances of John Fowles.* Basingstoke: Macmillan.

Mansfield, Elizabeth (1981) 'A Sequence of Endings: The Manuscripts of *The French Lieutenant's Woman*.' *Journal of Modern Literature*, 8:2: 275–86.

Olshen, Barry N. (1978) *John Fowles*. New York: Frederick Ungar.

Olshen, Barry N. and Olshen, Toni A. (1980) *John Fowles: A Reference Guide*. Boston, MA: G. K. Hall.

Onega, Susana (1989) *Form and Meaning in the Novels of John Fowles*. Ann Arbor, MI, London: UMI Research Press.

Palmer, William J. (1974) *The Fiction of John Fowles: Tradition, Art and the Loneliness of Selfhood*. Columbia: University of Missouri Press.

Rankin, Elizabeth D. (1973) 'Cryptic Coloration in *The French Lieutenant's Woman*'. *Journal of Narrative Technique*, 3: 193–207.

Rose, Gilbert J. (1972) '*The French Lieutenant's Woman*: The Unconscious Significance of a Novel to its Author'. *American Imago*, 29 (Summer): 165–76.

Ross, Suzanne (1999) ' "Water out of a Woodland Spring": Sarah Woodruff and Nature in *The French Lieutenant's Woman*', in James R. Aubrey (ed), *John Fowles and Nature: Fourteen Perspectives on Landscape*. London: Associated University Presses, pp. 181–94.

Salami, Mahmoud (1992) *John Fowles's Fiction and the Poetics of Postmodernism*. London and Toronto: Associated University Presses.

Stephenson, William (2003) *Writers and their Work: John Fowles*. Tavistock: Northcote House.

Tarbox, Katherine (1989) *The Art of John Fowles*. Athens, GA: University of Georgia Press.

Tucker, Stephanie (1996) 'Despair Not, Neither to Presume: *The French Lieutenant's Woman:* A Screenplay'. *Literature and Film Quarterly*, 24:1: 63–9.

Warburton, Eileen (1999) 'The Corpse in the Combe: The Vision of the Dead Woman in the Landscapes of John Fowles', in James R. Aubrey (ed), *John Fowles and Nature: Fourteen Perspectives on Landscape*. London: Associated University Presses, pp. 114–36.

Warburton, Eileen (2004) *John Fowles: A Life in Two Worlds*. London: Jonathan Cape.

Wolfe, Peter (1979) *John Fowles, Magus and Moralist* (second edition, revised). London: Associated University Presses.

Woodcock, Bruce (1984) *Male Mythologies: John Fowles and Masculinity*. Brighton: Harvester Press.

Other secondary works

Arnold, Matthew (1948) *Culture and Anarchy*. Ed. J. Dover Wilson. Cambridge: Cambridge University Press.

Arnold, Matthew (1950) *The Poetical Works of Matthew Arnold*. Ed. C. B. Tinker and H. F. Lowry. London, New York, Toronto: Oxford University Press.

Bakhtin, Mikhail (1981) *The Dialogic Imagination: Four Essays*. Ed. Michael Holquist. Trans. Caryl Emerson and Michael Holquist. Austin, TX: University of Texas Press.

Barthes, Roland (1977) *Image-Music-Text*. Trans. Stephen Heath. London: Fontana.

Barthes, Roland (1983) *Barthes: Selected Writings*. Ed. Susan Sontag. London: Fontana.

Baudrillard, Jean (1994) *Simulacra and Simulation*. Trans. Sheila Faria Glaser. Ann Arbor, MI: University of Michigan Press.

Belsey, Catherine (1980) *Critical Practice*. London and New York: Methuen.

Bradbury, Malcolm (1971) *The Social Context of Modern English Literature*. Oxford: Blackwell.

Brecht, Bertolt (1974) *Brecht on Theatre* (second edition). Ed. and trans. John Willett. London: Eyre Methuen.

Byatt, A. S. (1991) *Possession: A Romance*. London: Vintage.

Byatt, A. S. (2001) *On Histories and Stories: Selected Essays*. Cambridge, MA.: Harvard University Press.

Darwin, Charles (1985) *The Origin of Species*. Ed. J. W. Burrow. Harmondsworth: Penguin.

Eliot, George (1985) *The Mill on the Floss*. Ed. A. S. Byatt. London: Penguin.

Foucault, Michel (1990) *The History of Sexuality, Volume One: An Introduction*. Trans. Robert Hurley. Harmondsworth: Penguin.

Hardy, Thomas (1964) *The Well-Beloved: A Sketch of a Temperament*. London: Macmillan.

Hegel, Georg (1956) *The Philosophy of History*. Ed. C. J. Friedrich. Trans. J. Sibree. New York: Dover Publications.

Holloway, John (1953) *The Victorian Sage: Studies in Argument*. London: Macmillan.

Hutcheon, Linda (1988) *A Poetics of Postmodernism: History, Theory, Fiction*. London: Routledge.

Jameson, Fredric (1991) *Postmodernism, Or, the Cultural Logic of Late Capitalism*. London: Verso.

Joyce, James (2000) *A Portrait of the Artist as a Young Man*. Ed. Jeri Johnson. Oxford: Oxford University Press.

Kapur, Shekhar (dir.) (1998) *Elizabeth*. Channel 4 Films. Starring Cate Blanchett, Geoffrey Rush, Christopher Eccleston, Joseph Fiennes, Richard Attenborough. Screenplay by Michael Hirst.

Kermode, Frank (1975) *The Classic*. London: Faber.

Kermode, Frank (1983) *Essays on Fiction 1971–82*. London, Melbourne and Henley: Routledge and Kegan Paul.

Lawrence, D. H. (1993) *Sons and Lovers*. Ware: Wordsworth.

Lyotard, Jean-François (1984) *The Postmodern Condition: A Report on Knowledge*. Trans. Geoff Bennington and Brian Massumi. Foreword by Fredric Jameson. Manchester: University of Manchester Press.

Marx, Karl (1975) *Early Writings*. Ed. Lucio Colletti. Trans. Rodney Livingstone and Gregor Benton. Harmondsworth: Penguin.

McLuhan, Marshall (2001) *Understanding Media*. London: Routledge.

Monaco, James (2000) *How To Read a Film: Movies, Media, Multimedia* (third edition). Oxford: Oxford University Press.

Morris, Desmond (1968) *The Naked Ape*. London: Corgi.

Mulvey, Laura (1975) 'Visual Pleasure in Narrative Cinema'. *Screen*, 16:3 (Autumn): 6–18.

Pinter, Harold (1981) *The French Lieutenant's Woman: A Screenplay*. Boston, MA, Toronto: Little Brown.

Pyke, E. Royston (ed) (1967) *Human Documents of the Victorian Golden Age*. London: George Allen and Unwin.

Roof, Judith (1993) *A Lure of Knowledge: Lesbian Sexuality and Theory*. New York: Columbia University Press.

Roof, Judith (1996) *Come as You Are: Sexuality and Narrative*. New York: Columbia University Press.

Said, Edward (1991) *The World, the Text, and the Critic*. London: Vintage.

Sinfield, Alan (2004) *Literature, Politics and Culture in Postwar Britain*. London, New York: Continuum.

Villasur, Belén Vidal (2002) 'Classic adaptations, modern reinventions: reading the image in the contemporary literary film'. *Screen*, 43:1 (Spring): 5–18.

INDEX